BEFORE THE
GERANIUMS DIE

By
Hayden D. Wilson
Robert L. Williams

MSS Information Corporation
655 Madison Avenue, New York, N. Y. 10021

Library of Congress Catalog Card Number: 73-7159

Wilson, Hayden D. and Williams, Robert L.
    Before the geraniums die. a primer for
classroom management.
New York   MSS Information Corporation

May 1973   4-16,1973

The robins sang and sang and sang,
but teacher you went right on.
The last bell sounded the end of the day,
but teacher you went right on.
The geranium on the window sill just died,
but teacher you went right on.

Teacher, I guess you won.

Albert Cullum
The Geranium on the Window
Sill Just Died But Teacher
Went Right On
1971

CONTENTS

You are about to embark on a scintillating, enlightening, and, at times, inspiring exploration of classroom behavior management. Now, how can we possibly make such an outrageous claim? Well, because . . .

the authors have invested incredible effort in the
preparation of the manuscript, . . .

with occasional help from the secretaries--and after all...

preliminary student response does indicate that the
book will be widely "helled."

PROLOGUE

Until recently, educators have bombarded their colleagues with how to teach books that stress the need to "inspire" and "motivate" the learner, to "show" him the joys of learning, and to "captivate" his imagination. Though these are desirable goals, the majority of publications have been conspicuously lacking in precise directions for achieving these objectives. Instructions for the classroom teacher have often been in the form of such aphorisms as "provide fascinating and new materials," "be interesting," "don't let things get out of hand," or "be firm but fair." Again, these declarations represent sound advice, yet they rarely communicate any information which the teacher did not intuitively possess. More to the point, they do not really provide the teacher with any concrete advice on how to cope with thirty indifferent and often very disruptive students.

Recently, however, a number of books have been published which provide specific techniques for guiding classroom behaviors. This text is an extension of these efforts. An attempt is made in the current text to provide the teacher with some of the concrete skills necessary for effective classroom management. Basic concepts are explained and numerous examples of their implementation are provided. Because of the semi-programmed format of the text, readers must choose appropriate techniques and apply them to simulated classroom situations. Objectives are stated and post-tests are provided for each section of the text.

Most of the material which is included is applicable at both the elementary and secondary levels. However, particular emphasis is given to techniques of management appropriate for the much neglected secondary school environment. In addition, though most behavior modification material has dealt with individual students, the majority of the skills in this text are appropriate for group work as well. Some of these techniques are specifically applicable to the class as a whole.

The text is divided into two major parts. The first section, on positive reinforcement of desired behavior, is devoted to the effects of teacher attention on student behavior. Types of appropriate student responses and ways to reinforce these responses are indicated. Emphasis is given to ways in which the teacher can strengthen class-room behavior by more effective communication of his approval to the student. The second section is an attempt to provide the teacher with the skills to cope with class-room problems ranging from the little girl who is afraid to participate in class activities to the student who threatens his teacher or his peers with a weapon. A few of the other incidents dealt with are loud talking, cheat-ing, tattling, wandering around the room, and refusing to co-operate with teacher directions. Techniques for weakening undesirable behaviors are introduced and the situational variables which dictate or proscribe their implementation are examined.

Though it is often assumed that behavior management in the classroom implies that the students keep "stiff backs and straight rows," this text is not an endorsement of that policy. Based on the needs of his students, each educator should utilize this methodology to attain his own teaching objectives. The words "appropriate" and "inappropriate" used throughout the text can be defined only in terms of the individual classroom. Appropriate responses for a student might vary from coming to class on time to formulating his own classroom objectives and working on them independently. Therefore, most of the procedures presented here can be implemented in both traditional and non-conventional learning environments.

We wish to express our appreciation to Lana Arms and to Emily Blake for their enormous patience in typing this manuscript. We are also grateful to Debra Curde for the cartoon work.

"Weird" behaviors are not necessarily incompatible with academic productivity, i.e., just because you don't work this way doesn't mean that they can't--or shouldn't.

SECTION I

POSITIVE REINFORCEMENT OF DESIRED BEHAVIOR

OBJECTIVES:

(1) You will be able to define a positive reinforcer, stating that it is a stimulus which strengthens the response which precedes it.

(2) You will be able to enumerate three types of student reactions which should be positively reinforced. These are:
    (a) specific responses
    (b) certain categories of responses
    (c) the positive feelings that underlie appropriate behavior

(3) You will be able to write at least two comments which would positively reinforce the learner for <u>each</u> of the three types of pupil reactions.

(4) You will be able to write at least four comments which would positively reinforce a student for attempting to answer a question even though he has given an incorrect answer.

(5) You will be able to write, without prompts, the five rules for using positive reinforcers. They are:
    (a) Reinforce small steps at first.
    (b) Give frequent reinforcement to establish a behavior and intermittent reinforcement to maintain it.
    (c) Make your reinforcement contingent on the desired behavior.
    (d) Give your reinforcement immediately after the desired behavior.
    (e) Be consistent.

(6) Given a classroom situation in which a teacher is attempting to modify a student's behavior by the use of positive reinforcement, you will be able to point out errors in the teacher's application of this concept. The errors will involve breaking one or more of the five rules of positive reinforcement.

14

(7)   Given a classroom situation in which one or more students are exhibiting undesirable behavior, you will be
able to describe how to use positive reinforcement to
effect some desired change in the student's behavior.

WHAT IS POSITIVE REINFORCEMENT?

Positive reinforcement is the presentation of some
stimulus (e.g., praise, candy, tokens) which strengthens
the response which precedes it. We often refer to these
kinds of stimuli as rewards. Thus, you might strengthen
a desired behavior (completing work assignments) from a
third grader by giving him a small piece of candy (reward or
positive reinforcement) for each completed assignment.

What is positively reinforcing will vary somewhat from
person to person and from time to time for the same person.
A small piece of candy might be a positive reinforcer for a
first grader but not for a seventh grader. Reading comic
books might be positively reinforcing to one seventh grader,
but not to another. Also, reading comic books might
initially be reinforcing to a seventh grader, but lose much
of its reinforcement value after several weeks. Therefore,
to positively reinforce a child, you must find something
that he likes or wants to do at that point in time. It may
not be sufficient to use as reinforcers those things that
you enjoy doing or things the child enjoyed several weeks
ago.

Of the classroom stimuli which are potentially reinforcing, teacher attention and success feedback appear to
be reinforcing to the greatest number of children. We have
found that students from kindergarten through graduate
school seem to respond positively to these events. Conse-
quently, this booklet will focus mainly upon the use of
these stimuli in modifying behavior. Two other categories
of reinforcers, tangible payoffs and free time activities,
will be treated in less detail.

(1)   Which of the following would probably be positive
reinforcers for primary school children?
      (a)   praise
      (b)   candy
      (c)   harsh, angry words
      (d)   indifference
      (e)   special privileges

*a,b,e

(2) However, what might be a positive reinforcer for one
person _____ be rewarding to another.

*might not

(3) When you choose a positive reinforcer for changing a
student's behavior, you should choose something that
(you, the student) _____ likes or enjoys.

*the student

(4) Attention serves as a _____ for most students.

*positive reinforcer

(5) Since teacher attention can be such a powerful reinforcer, a student who does poor work might actually do
poorer work after the teacher has given him a lecture
on how well he should be doing and how capable he is.
In this case the _____ could be a positive reinforcer for doing poor work.

*lecture

(6) If a student spells a word correctly during an oral
spelling test and you commend him in front of the class,
he will probably work (more, less) _____ on his
next spelling test.

*more

(7) Likewise, if you smile at a student when he is making
an undesirable response, you are probably reinforcing
the _____ behavior.

*undesired

(8) If a teacher dismisses a class early because it is
getting too noisy, we would expect the noisy behavior
to _____ because it is being positively reinforced by the class's being _____.

*increase
dismissed early

Reinforcement preferences do vary across individuals.

(9) Social reinforcement is probably the most common form
of positive reinforcement. Smiles, hugs, nods, verbal
recognition, and pats on the shoulder are all forms
of _____.

*social reinforcement

(10) Even the worst students make some desirable responses.
The idea is not to force yourself to praise anything
and everything, but rather to make an effort to notice
a student whenever he makes _____ responses.

*desirable

(11) If a student who only occasionally turns in assignments
does his assignment today, which of the following
comments would be appropriate?
(a) "This is the BEST work that I have ever seen!"
(b) "So you finally decided to do some work?"
(c) "You really did some work last night!"
(d) "If you complete the next 15 assignments you MIGHT
be able to pass this session."

*c

(12) Any social reinforcement should be realistic. If a
learner knows that he is barely getting by, he will
distrust comments like "You are the smartest person in
this whole class." A comment such as _____ in
frame 11 is equally unrealistic.

*a

(13) Anyone should be able to sincerely tell a student that
he is pleased the student's work is improving. However,
when a teacher either repeats a response such as "good"
all day long or couches her responses in grandiose
terms, the students tend to doubt the _____
of the teacher's compliments. Hence, the student is
more likely to perceive your verbal approval as sincere if it _____ and if it is not _____.

*sincerity
 varies
 grandiose, extreme

18

(14) Other cues are important in communicating the sincerity of your approval to the student. Your facial expression and the tone of your voice are both important. Which of the following would the learner probably interpret as being more sincere?
(a) "That is better" accompanied by a smile.
(b) "Excellent, excellent" spoken in a hurried manner and without any facial expression.

*a

(15) Since most students have had so little experience with praise in the school system, some might be skeptical of your sincerity at first. However, if you pair your approval with something which the student already enjoys, it will become far more potent. For example, you might say "This is an excellent paper. You made an A on it," or "Excellent," and then give the student points or tokens which may be traded in for some prearranged reward. Thus, pairing your approval with something which is already a _____ will make your approval more potent.

*positive reinforcer

WHAT TYPES OF RESPONSES SHOULD BE REINFORCED?

The first of the three types of pupil reactions which should be reinforced is specific responses. For instance, you might reinforce a student for giving a correct answer, turning in an assignment, or writing a good paper. Several comments which might be helpful in providing positive feedback for specific responses are: "Excellent," "Very good," "I could tell that you put some effort into this one," "I'm glad that you did that," "Thanks," "I like that," "I'm pleased that you turned this in."

(1) Write two more comments which you might wish to use to reinforce specific responses.
(a)
(b)

*"This is more like it."
"This is by far the best you have done."
"You're exactly right."

(2)   In addition to reinforcing students for the specific responses they make, a teacher should attempt to reinforce students for <u>certain</u> <u>categories</u> <u>of</u> <u>responses</u>, e.g., asking questions, answering questions, expressing opinions. In this case, instead of saying to a child, "I'm glad you asked that question," a teacher might say, "I'm glad you're asking questions." In attempting to reinforce a student for expressing his opinions, a teacher might say _____.

*"I'm glad you express your opinion."
 "I'm glad that you tell us how you feel."
 "It's nice that you speak up."

(3)   By attending to certain categories of responses you can reinforce a student for attempting to answer a question even though he has given a wrong answer. You might say "That isn't quite it, but you are getting close," or "It's nice that you've told us what you think. Does someone else have a different answer?" Another response might be _____.

*"I like to hear you state your opinion. Now let's see what Sally has to say."
 "That's not quite right, but if you keep thinking that hard you're going to come up with it."

(4)   Of the three types of student behaviors which you should reinforce, the two we have discussed thus far are _____ _____ and _____ _____ __ _____.

*specific responses
 certain categories of responses

(5)   A teacher should also attempt to reinforce the <u>positive</u> <u>feelings</u> <u>that</u> <u>underlie</u> <u>appropriate</u> <u>behavior</u>. For instance, instead of simply saying, "I'm glad you did that," the teacher might say, "I'm glad you seem to enjoy doing that." This strategy seems to be an especially potent way of conveying to the child that his happiness matters to you. If a teacher noticed that a child was smiling as he worked his math problems, he (the teacher) might say _____.

*"You looked like you really enjoyed solving those problems."
 "It's nice that you seem to enjoy math."

(6) Therefore, the three types of student reactions which should be reinforced are _____ _____, _____ _____ __ _____ , and _____ _____ _____ _____ _____.

*specific responses
 certain categories of responses
 positive feelings that underlie appropriate behavior

CORRECT AND INCORRECT APPLICATIONS OF POSITIVE REINFORCEMENT:

It is imperative that you be cognizant of how you are positively reinforcing students and what you are positively reinforcing. Few teachers deliberately reinforce inappropriate behavior. Yet inappropriate behavior is emitted at a very high rate in numerous classrooms. Apparently, many teachers fail to consistently reinforce appropriate behaviors and may inadvertently reinforce inappropriate behaviors.

(1) If a student raises his hand several times to answer a question and the teacher ignores him each time, the student will be _____ (more, less) likely to raise his hand in the future.

 *less

(2) If a student yells from the back of the room, "I know the answer," and the teacher then asks him for the answer, the yelling response is likely to be _____.

 *strengthened, reinforced

(3) If a student talks to neighbors, drops his books on the floor, and repeatedly sharpens his pencil, and the teacher then tells him "Go dust the erasers; just get out of my hair," the boisterous behavior is likely to be _____ because of the _____ of getting out of class.

 *strengthened
 positive reinforcement

21

(4) If a student volunteers to answer a question during class discussion, and the teacher tells him that he has given a stupid answer and assigns him extra work, it is _____ that this student will volunteer to answer any more questions.

*unlikely

(5) It seems that students work hard to elicit teacher attention. If positive attention is not accessible, then negative attention is usually preferred to no attention. Therefore, a major reason why students continue to emit high rates of inappropriate behavior is that such behavior pays off in eliciting teacher _____.

*attention

(6) If a teacher uses very little approval, her disapproval may become reinforcing. For example, if the teacher generally ignores Johnny while he is working at his seat but quickly reprimands him with comments such as "Sit down," "Go back to your seat," and "Get back to work" when he gets out of his seat, the number of times that Johnny gets out of his seat will likely _____.

*increase

(7) In contrast to the previous frame, if a teacher employs a great deal of approval and infrequent disapproval, her disapproval may serve as an effective deterrent to inappropriate behavior. Therefore, when a teacher consistently attends to and approves children for working at their seats, her disapproving a child for getting out of his seat will likely _____ out of seat behaviors.

*decrease

(8) There are many ways other than direct approval by which a teacher can reinforce appropriate student behavior. For example, in class discussion, a teacher need not always praise student comments to increase the frequency of students' speaking up. By restating students' comments or using them as the basis of further class discussion, the teacher will likely increase the frequency with which students ask or answer questions. If the teacher, following Johnny's

statement of his opinion, comments, "Johnny, your opinion seems to be that . . .", she will probably _____ Johnny for expressing his opinion.

*reinforce

RULES FOR USING REINFORCERS:

(A) REINFORCE SMALL STEPS AT FIRST.

Positively reinforce small improvements. Do not wait for perfection. A student who only occasionally does his English assignment should be positively reinforced for turning in an assignment. As he begins to do more work, be more selective in your reinforcement. For instance, after he has begun to turn in all of his assignments, praise only the better ones. This process is called SHAPING. The idea is to reward the learner as his behavior comes closer and closer to the desired behavior.

(1) Rewarding closer and closer approximations of a desired behavior is called _____.

*shaping

(2) As the rough approximations become more frequent you would reward only closer _____ of the behavior.

*approximations

(3) For example: It seems that your students are unable to sustain academic activities for extended time periods. You would like for them to be able to work without interruption for about 30 minutes. Presently, an interruption occurs almost every minute. In shaping their capacity to work for longer periods, you might begin by _____ them for working one minute. When it becomes obvious that they can work for one minute without interruption, you should then require them to work _____ before issuing reinforcement. As they are able to work longer, continue to raise your standards. However, never make your standards so high that students are rarely able to attain them. If you eventually get your students to the point that they can easily work 15 minutes without interruptions, you might then be tempted to try 30 minutes.

But if your students go two days without meeting the 30 minute criterion, you should _____ your standard.

*praising, reinforcing
 longer, 2 minutes
 lower

(4) Therefore, one rule for using reinforcers is to rein-force _____.

*small steps at first

(B) GIVE FREQUENT REINFORCEMENT TO ESTABLISH A BEHAVIOR AND INTERMITTENT REINFORCEMENT TO MAINTAIN IT.

If you want a student to volunteer more frequently to answer questions in class discussion (target behavior), begin by calling on him practically every time he raises his hand. After he has begun to volunteer quite often, you could call on him less frequently. Thus, a student learns a behavior (volunteering in class) by being positively rein-forced (given attention by the teacher) practically every time that he volunteers. But the behavior is maintained by his being called on only occasionally. However, it is not likely that the student will continue to volunteer answers indefinitely if you completely stop giving him attention.

Giving reinforcement each time that a behavior occurs is called a CONTINUOUS schedule of reinforcement. When you only occasionally reinforce responses, you are using an INTERMITTENT schedule of reinforcement.

(1) To establish a behavior you would use a _____ schedule of reinforcement. However, after the response occurs frequently, you would use an _____ schedule of reinforcement.

*continuous
 intermittent

(2) Intermittent reinforcement is useful in _____ behavior.

*maintaining

24

(3) If Johnny only occasionally turns in his homework, we should attempt to reinforce that behavior on a _____ schedule.

*continuous

(4) After Johnny has gotten to the point where he turns in homework practically every day, we should shift to an _____ schedule of reinforcement.

*intermittent

(5) A behavior that has been maintained through inter-mittent reinforcement will continue to be emitted much longer after the external reinforcer is withdrawn than one which has been maintained through continuous rein-forcement. Therefore, if Johnny's handraising has been maintained through intermittent teacher recog-nition, he will continue to raise his hand much longer after teacher recognition is totally withdrawn than if handraising had been maintained on a _____ schedule.

*continuous

(6) The transition from a continuous to a partial rein-forcement schedule should be made very gradually. Once you have gotten the behavior to an acceptable frequency via continuous reinforcement, perhaps the next step is to reinforce every other occurrence of the behavior. By gradually increasing the ratio, you will eventually be able to maintain the behavior with very infrequent reinforcement. If Johnny's handraising is being main-tained on a 1 to 10 ratio, the next step might be (1 to 12, 1 to 100) _____ ratio.

*1 to 12

(7) The two rules for using reinforcers which we have covered are: (a) _____
(b) Give frequent _____
_____
_____

*(a) Reinforce small steps at first.
 (b) Give frequent reinforcement to establish a behavior and intermittent reinforcement to main-tain it.

25

(C) MAKE YOUR REINFORCEMENT CONTINGENT UPON THE DESIRED
BEHAVIOR.

If you intend to praise a student for remaining in his
seat during the class period, praise him only if he is in
his seat. If you promise your class candy, free time, or
some privilege (positive reinforcers) for turning in their
book reports on time (desired behavior), then you should be
sure that you only give the positive reinforcers (your part
of the bargain) if they do the work on time (their part of
the bargain).

Contrast contingent reinforcement with rewards which
are given irrespective of what the child does. If Johnny
knows that he will get free time irrespective of whether
he completes his assignment, free time is not likely to act
as a reinforcer for completing his assignment. If Billy
knows that he will get his allowance irrespective of whether
he does his chores around the house, the allowance is not
likely to serve as a reinforcer for doing his chores.

(1) If you tell your students that each person must turn
in his book report to be allowed to go to the library
for the last half hour of class and then you permit a
student who has not completed his report to go, you
have _____ his NOT turning in a book
report. Will he work to earn the next privilege that
you offer? _____

*positively reinforced
no

(2) If you give positive reinforcement when a student is
exhibiting undesired behavior you have strengthened the
_____ behavior.

*undesired

(3) You should give positive reinforcement ONLY for _____
behaviors or for changes in the desired direction.

*desired

(4) Essentially, your reinforcement will strengthen what-
ever behaviors it is _____ upon.

*contingent

26

(5) However, you must look at contingencies from the
     child's perspective. You may intend to give free time
     only to those students who have completed their assign-
     ments. However, if Johnny gets free time without
     completing his assignment, then from his perspective
     free time is contingent upon _____ the
     assignment.

     *not completing

(6) Some teachers promise rewards for appropriate behavior
     when students begin to emit inappropriate behaviors.
     Suppose every time the class gets disruptive, Ms. Brown
     promises them an early recess if they will quieten
     down. By using this approach she will actually
     increase the frequency of _____ behavior.

     *disruptive

(7) Thus, three of the five rules for using reinforcers
     are:
     (a) _Reinforce small steps_
     (b) _Frequently reinforce to establish a desired_
          behavior + reinforce intermittally to maintain it.

     (c) Make your reinforcement _contingent on the desired behavior_
          _____ _____ _____ _____.

     *(a) Reinforce small steps at first.
      (b) Give frequent reinforcement to establish a
           behavior and intermittent reinforcement to main-
           tain it.
      (c) contingent upon the desired behavior

(D) GIVE YOUR REINFORCER IMMEDIATELY AFTER THE DESIRED
     BEHAVIOR.

     This is especially important with younger children.
Though some children are able to work for grades (delayed
positive reinforcers), immediate positive reinforcement is
MUCH more effective. If students are working diligently on
assigned work, then tell them that they are doing a good job.
GIVE FEEDBACK TO YOUR STUDENTS: IF THEY ARE DOING WELL, LET
THEM KNOW IT THEN AND THERE. Do not depend on a report card
every six weeks to do your work for you. If a normally
boisterous child goes through even one of your classes
without an outburst, make a point of telling him immediately
that you noticed how well he did and that you appreciate it.

(1) Feedback on appropriate behavior should be as _____ as possible.

*immediate

(2) One problem with grades is that there is too much _____ between the behavior and the _____.

*delay, time
 feedback

(3) If grades were given immediately after an assignment was completed they would be _____ effective.

*more

(4) A football coach frequently told his players in the dressing room following practice how well they had done during the practice session. His praise would have been more effective had it been issued during practice _____ after a player executed a play properly.

*immediately

(5) The four rules covered so far are:
 (a) _____
 (b) _____
     _____
 (c) _____
     _____
 (d) Give your reinforcer _____
     _____.

*(a) Reinforce small steps at first.
 (b) Give frequent reinforcement to establish a behavior and intermittent reinforcement to maintain it.
 (c) Make your reinforcement contingent upon the desired behavior.
 (d) immediately after the desired behavior.

(E) BE CONSISTENT.

Some teachers are quite inconsistent from day to day and from student to student in terms of how they respond to student behaviors. One day a student may be approved for a particular behavior and the next day be reprimanded for essentially the same behavior. One student may be recognized only if he raises his hand and another may get the floor by yelling at the teacher. Teachers who vascillate from day to day and student to student are likely to be characterized by students as unfair and moody. At any rate, such inconsistency limits the effectiveness of a behavior management system.

The type of inconsistency referred to in the previous paragraph is not to be confused with the irregularity of an intermittent reinforcement schedule. Under intermittent reinforcement, students come to recognize that every appropriate response will not be reinforced. However, behaving appropriately will evenutally result in reinforcement. So a teacher is consistent in that she only provides reinforcement for appropriate behaviors.

(1) If a teacher reccgnizes a student one time for raising his hand and the next time for yelling, the student may subsequently emit _____ behavior in attempting to get the teacher's attention.

*either

(2) If a teacher smiles at Johnny today for making a witty remark and tomorrow chastises him for making a similar remark, Johnny is likely to conclude that the teacher's response is more a function of her _____ than of his behavior.

*mood

(3) If a teacher is consistent in what she reinforces, students will likely conclude that it is their _____ and not the teacher's _____ that determines when reinforcement is given.

*behavior
  mood

(4) Therefore, the five rules for using reinforcers are:
  (a) _____
  (b) _____
      _____
      _____
  (c) _____
      _____
      _____

(d) _____

(e) Be _____

*(a) Reinforce small steps at first.
 (b) Give frequent reinforcement to establish a
     behavior and intermittent reinforcement to main-
     tain it.
 (c) Make your reinforcement contingent upon the desired
     behavior.
 (d) Give your reinforcer immediately after the desired
     behavior.
 (e) Be consistent.

THINK ABOUT THE FOLLOWING INCIDENT IN TERMS OF WHAT YOU HAVE
LEARNED ABOUT POSITIVE REINFORCEMENT.

After learning from other teachers about the use of
positive reinforcers, Mrs. Hann decided to use candy as a
positive reinforcer to develop the reading skill of 2nd
graders. She carefully explained to them that for each five
pages that they read aloud in reading groups they would be
given a piece of candy at the end of the week. Accordingly,
each day she conscientiously wrote in her grade book the
number of pieces of candy due each student. However, only a
few students read more throughout the week. Most only did
an increased amount of reading on Friday. In addition, the
poorer readers seemed to get worse.

WHICH OF THE FOLLOWING ERRORS DID MRS. HANN MAKE IN APPLYING
THE CONCEPT OF POSITIVE REINFORCEMENT?
(Choose one or more of the following; answers are on the
 next page)

(a) She explained the contingencies.

(b) She was not consistent.

(c) The steps were too large for some students.

(d) The reinforcement was not immediate.

(e) Candy was not a good positive reinforcer.

(f) While candy is a positive reinforcer for 2nd graders,
    it cannot be used to upgrade reading skills.

ANSWER

c,d

EXPLANATION:

(a) In many cases (e.g., handraising, staying in seat, improving quality of work) you may or may not choose to tell the student what the contingencies are (If your paper is 90% correct, THEN you will be given ten minutes of free time at the end of the period). Contingency management works either way, but an overt explanation of the desirable and undesirable consequencies of the behavior is preferred by most teachers.

(b) Apparently, she was consistent. Each day she recorded the students' accomplishments in her gradebook.

(c) Probably most of the students could easily read more than five pages. However, the poor students might do well to read five pages correctly in two weeks. There should have been some individualization in the required material. All students should be given achievable goals. Learning is facilitated by successful completion of work and hampered by repeated experiences of failure. Initially, the slower students might have to read only one page to earn a piece of candy. As they become more proficient, you would require more work from them.

(d) No--it wasn't. It would have been far more effective to either give the candy to the student as soon as he met the criterion, to give points on a large board prominently displayed, or to give tokens. At the end of the week the points or tokens could be swapped for the candy. It is particularly important to give younger children immediate feedback concerning their work.

(e) Candy is usually quite reinforcing for 2nd graders.

(f) Candy has been used very successfully to upgrade the reading skills of primary school students.

FOR THE FOLLOWING INCIDENT, IDENTIFY HOW YOU WOULD USE THE
PRINCIPLES OF POSITIVE REINFORCEMENT TO HELP JOHN COMPLETE
HIS ASSIGNMENTS.

John Speed, a student in your 7th grade class, day-
dreams a lot. He stares out the window, at the chalkboard,
or just out into space. He seldom completes assignments,
and often doesn't even start. Though his grades are very
poor, you believe that he is capable of at least average
work.

(A) REINFORCE SMALL STEPS AT FIRST.

You might praise John whenever he completes an assignment. However, he rarely completes assignments. Therefore,
it would probably be better to begin by positively reinforcing him any time that he appears to be working on an
assignment. Your praise might be nothing more than saying
"That looks good, John," or "At this rate, you should be
finished in no time at all." As time goes on, require that
he sit in his seat and work for a longer period of time
before you issue your approval.

(B) GIVE FREQUENT REINFORCEMENT TO ESTABLISH A BEHAVIOR AND
    INTERMITTENT REINFORCEMENT TO MAINTAIN IT.

At first you would praise John every time that you
observe him working. However, as he begins to spend more
time on his assignments your praise would be given at
greater intervals. If he is able to work all period without
daydreaming, you might want to recognize his hard work only
every other day. After the behavior is well-established,
you must still reinforce good work, but you do not have to
reinforce it every time that it occurs.

(C) MAKE YOUR REINFORCEMENT CONTINGENT ON THE DESIRED
    BEHAVIOR.

Only praise him when he is working. Do not pay attention to him when he is not performing the desired behavior.

(D) GIVE YOUR REINFORCEMENT IMMEDIATELY AFTER THE DESIRED
    BEHAVIOR.

Don't observe John working and praise him the next day.
Praise him while he is working or immediately after he completes his work.

(E)   BE CONSISTENT.

Don't praise John's work today and make a sarcastic remark about it tomorrow.

POST-TEST OVER POSITIVE REINFORCEMENT OF DESIRED BEHAVIORS.

(1)   What is a positive reinforcer?

(2)   Enumerate three types of student responses which should be positively reinforced.
      (a)
      (b)
      (c)

(3)   Write two positively reinforcing comments for each of the three types of student responses.
      (a)
      (b)

      (a)
      (b)

      (a)
      (b)

(4)   Suzie is smiling while working on her art project. An appropriate response to Suzie would be:
      (a)   "Wipe that smile off your face."
      (b)   "Why don't you get to work on something important?"
      (c)   "I'm glad that you seem to enjoy your art work."
      (d)   "I'm glad you're working on your art project."

(5)   Write four comments which would likely reinforce a student for attempting to answer a question even though he has given an incorrect answer.
      (a)
      (b)
      (c)
      (d)

(6) What are the five rules for using positive reinforcers?
   (a)
   (b)
   (c)
   (d)
   (e)

(7) If a student continues to make sarcastic comments during class even though the teacher repeatedly tells him not to, we might conclude
   (a) that either teacher or peer attention is reinforcing the behavior.
   (b) that he's a bad boy.
   (c) that there is more reinforcement for emitting the behavior than there is for being quiet.
   (d) that the teacher should call him down more.
   (e) Both a and c.

(8) Miss Jones is trying to help Bill, a very poor speller, improve his spelling, i.e., to raise the percentage of words which he spells correctly on each quiz. While collecting the assignments, she sees that he has spelled four out of twelve words (33 1/3%) correctly. He normally only gets about 10% correct. What would be the most appropriate comment for her to make?
   (a) "Bill, this is one of the best papers that I have ever seen."
   (b) "I am gratified by your splendid improvement in this endeavor."
   (c) "Good, Bill - you did quite a bit better today."
   (d) "This isn't bad for a dummy."
   (e) "This is an excellent paper."

(9) Ms. Smith was attempting to use tangible rewards to get her students to behave appropriately. When the noise level began to mount in the room she would promise her students candy if they would quieten down. She subsequently found that the frequency of noisy behavior increased. She was obviously breaking which of the five rules of positive reinforcement?

(10) Mr. Stern was attempting to use approval to increase appropriate student behaviors. On most days, he frequently and immediately approved students for making appropriate responses. However, on other days it seemed that Mr. Stern was in a bad mood, because he responded sarcastically to almost anything the students

said. Which of the five rules of positive reinforcement was he breaking?

(11) Sally is a frail-looking little girl with a timid laugh and a cautious smile. Her work is about average. When you call on her she can usually answer the question but she never volunteers. She is just one of those kids that you never really notice. BUT YOU SHOULD!

How would you apply positive reinforcement of desired behavior to increase Sally's rate of volunteering? It is not necessary to justify your work; just be sure that you follow the five rules.

SECTION II

TECHNIQUES FOR WEAKENING INAPPROPRIATE BEHAVIOR

OBJECTIVES:

(1) After reading the introductory section you will be able to write the four rules for weakening undesirable behavior. They are:
  (a) Use the appropriate strategy immediately following the behavior to be weakened.
  (b) Be consistent.
  (c) Direct your response at specific student behaviors --not at the student himself.
  (d) Reinforce desired behavior.

(2) After you have finished all of the units on the techniques for weakening undesirable behaviors, you will be able to write the definition of each of these techniques.

(3) After you have finished all of the units, you will be able to describe under what circumstances each of these five techniques should be used.

(4) After you have finished all of the units, you will be able to identify at least three behaviors which could be dealt with by each of the techniques for weakening inappropriate behaviors.

(5) After you have completed each of the units you will be able to apply the four rules for weakening behavior in the following ways:
  (a) Given a classroom situation in which a teacher is attempting to weaken undesirable behavior by using one or more of the specified techniques, you will be able to point out errors in the teacher's strategy. The classroom situations will include:
    (1) Destruction of property
    (2) Refusing to comply with teacher directions
    (3) Tardiness
    (4) Arguing
  (b) Given a classroom situation in which one or more students are exhibiting undesirable behavior, you will be able to describe how to effect a positive

change in the students' behavior. The classroom situations will include:
(1) Fighting
(2) Using profanity
(3) Excessive noise
(4) Throwing objects

GUIDELINES FOR WEAKENING INAPPROPRIATE BEHAVIOR

Five major behavior management techniques, reinforcement of behavior which is incompatible with the undesired behavior, extinction, time-out, response cost, and punishment, are directed at weakening undesirable academic and social behaviors. It is unlikely that you will use any of these techniques to the exclusion of the others. All of them should be important parts of your contingency management program and each should be used with the types of behaviors for which they are most appropriate. However, regardless of the method which you use to weaken behaviors, you should utilize the following rules:

(A) RESPOND IMMEDIATELY TO THE UNDESIRED BEHAVIOR.

(1) Whether you are attempting to strengthen or weaken certain behaviors, your reaction should be as _____ as possible.

*immediate

(2) If you want to discourage a student from chewing gum but wait until he raises his hand to answer a question before commenting on his gum chewing, it is <u>possible</u> that you will weaken gum chewing behavior, but it is more likely that you will weaken the behavior of

_____.

*volunteering to answer questions

(3) Regardless of the grade level of the student, the more immediate your reaction to an inappropriate behavior, the greater the probability that it will be associated with the student's undesirable behavior. Telling a high school student that you are displeased with something that he did two weeks ago is less effective than telling him _____ would have been, and telling a third grader that you are not pleased with something that he did last week is almost totally _____ in weakening that behavior.

* immediately
  ineffective

(4) Therefore, one rule for weakening inappropriate behaviors is to respond _____.

*immediately to the undesired behavior

(B) BE CONSISTENT.

(1) If you tell students that their behavior will have certain consequences, then you must enforce these consequences. If you have a rule which states that "anyone who cheats will lose his free time for two days", enforce it EACH time that you catch students cheating. Do not give warnings, make threats, or say "The next time that you cheat, you . . ." Just make your rules clear and enforce them _____.

*consistently

(2) If students find that they can talk you out of giving them a bad grade, you have _____ them for arguing and haven't punished them for anything. So in addition to the behavior for which you gave them a bad grade, you now have a new inappropriate behavior, _____, with which to deal.

*reinforced
  arguing with the teacher

(3) A golf pro who can't be consistent in swinging at the ball won't be able to control where the ball goes, and the teacher who cannot be consistent in dealing with her pupils will have no control over their _____.

*behavior

(4) The two rules for weakening inappropriate behavior which we have covered are:
    (a) _____.
    (b) Be _____.

*(a) Respond immediately to the undesirable behavior
 (b) consistent

39

(C) DIRECT YOUR RESPONSE AT SPECIFIC STUDENT BEHAVIORS
--NOT AT THE STUDENT HIMSELF

(1) When a student disrupts your class by wandering around the room, coming in late, and talking out, he is exhibiting three specific _____ which you might wish to weaken.

*behaviors

(2) These three behaviors should not be interpreted as symptoms of a character or personality disorder. Instead, they should be viewed simply as three behaviors which are _____ for your classroom environment.

*inappropriate, maladaptive

(3) When it is necessary to respond verbally to one of these behaviors, you should respond in terms of what the student has done. For example, "Bob, your loud talking is . . .," or "Bill, you didn't bring a notebook or a pencil to class, so . . ." A remark such as "Priscilla, I just don't understand what is wrong with you." is inappropriate because it does not deal with

_____.

*specific behavior

(4) Since a remark such as "Can't you do anything right"? or "Don't you know right from wrong"? attacks someone's character, we would expect it to weaken _____.

*character, self-concept

(5) Thus, teacher reactions should not impugn the student's _____ but should be directed at _____

_____.

*character, integrity
 specific behaviors

(6) Thus, three of the four rules for using reinforcers are:
(a) _____.
(b) _____.
(c) Direct _____.

40

*(a) Respond . . .
 (b) Be . . .
 (c) your response at specific student behaviors - not
      at the student himself

(D) REINFORCE DESIRED BEHAVIOR

(1) Regardless of the technique which you are utilizing to
     weaken undesirable behaviors, it is essential that you
     reinforce desired behaviors simultaneously. It is not
     enough to discourage someone from doing what you feel
     is inappropriate; you must also provide encourage-
     ment for what you feel is _____.

     *appropriate

(2) To avoid punishment (bad grades, teacher disapproval),
     the student can cheat, quit school, or do satisfactory
     work. It is up to the teacher to make sure that doing
     satisfactory work is the most _____ of these
     very real alternatives.

     *reinforcing

(3) Therefore, the four rules for weakening inappropriate
     behavior are:
     (a) _____.
     (b) _____.
     (c) _____.
     (d) Reinforce _____.

     *(a) Respond . . .
      (b) Be . . .
      (c) Direct . . .
      (d) desired behavior

TECHNIQUE I: REINFORCEMENT OF BEHAVIOR INCOMPATIBLE WITH
THE UNDESIRED BEHAVIOR

OBJECTIVES:

(1) You will be able to define an incompatible behavior as
a behavior which cannot be performed at the same time
as another behavior.

(2) You will be able to tell under what circumstances you
should use reinforcement of incompatible behavior to
weaken undesired behavior.

(3) You will be able to give three examples of student
behaviors which could be dealt with by reinforcement
of incompatible behaviors.

(4) Given a classroom situation in which a teacher is
attempting to modify a student's behavior by reinforcement of incompatible behavior, you will be able to
point out errors in the teacher's application of this
concept. The errors could be either:
(a) Breaking one or more of the five rules for using
reinforcers
(b) Breaking one or more of the four rules for weakening inappropriate behavior
(c) Reinforcing behavior which is not incompatible
with the undesired behavior

(5) Given a classroom situation in which one or more
students are exhibiting undesirable behavior, you will
be able to describe how to use the technique of reinforcing incompatible behavior to effect some desired
change in the students' behavior.

WHAT ARE INCOMPATIBLE BEHAVIORS?

(1) Incompatible behaviors are behaviors which are difficult to perform at the same time. Coming to school
and being absent are incompatible. Working on an
assignment is incompatible with pulling Ann's hair,
passing notes, stealing, and innumerable other disruptions. Failing to pay attention is incompatible with
_____.

*paying attention

42

(2)   To keep a student from emitting an undesirable behav-
      ior, strengthen a desirable behavior which is
      incompatible with the undesirable behavior. If you
      don't want a student to stand up, then reinforce him
      for sitting. He certainly can't do both simultan-
      eously, and your reinforcement should make _____
      the more desirable of the two alternatives. Likewise,
      if a student talks too much, you might reinforce him
      when _____ .

      *sitting
       he isn't talking

(3)   If Mary comes in late to class several days a week, the
      behavior incompatible with coming in late would be
      _____ .

      *coming in early or on time

(4)   To keep students from coming to your desk to ask
      questions, you might reinforce them for _____
      _____ .

      *staying in their seats and raising their hands

WHEN SHOULD YOU USE REINFORCEMENT OF BEHAVIOR INCOMPATIBLE
WITH THE UNDESIRED BEHAVIOR?

(1)   When you reinforce behavior which is incompatible with
      the undesired behavior you are reinforcing a specific
      form of _____ behavior which cannot be
      performed at the same time as a specific _____
      behavior.

      *desired
       undesired

(2)   When attempting to weaken any kind of undesirable
      behavior, you should attempt to reinforce the behavior
      which is incompatible with that specific inappropriate
      behavior. Thus, you should attempt to strengthen
      _____ whenever you are
      attempting to weaken any undesirable behaviors, regard-
      less of the other method which you might use in
      conjunction with this technique.

      *incompatible behaviors

THINK ABOUT THE FOLLOWING INCIDENT IN TERMS OF WHAT YOU HAVE
LEARNED ABOUT REINFORCEMENT OF BEHAVIOR INCOMPATIBLE WITH
THE UNDESIRED BEHAVIOR

Ms. Dimples is attempting to use the method of reinforcement of incompatible behaviors to keep Heathcliff from
wandering around the room so much. Though Heathcliff never
bothers his classmates, he rarely finishes his work and his
wandering irritates Ms. Dimples. Each time that he gets
out of his seat she goes over to him and asks him to sit
down. As soon as he is seated, she compliments him on something that he has done. But alas, it isn't working.

WHAT ERROR DID MS. DIMPLES MAKE IN APPLYING THE CONCEPT OF
INCOMPATIBLE BEHAVIORS?

(Hint: She has either broken one of the rules for using
reinforcers or one of the rules for weakening undesirable
behaviors.)

DON'T KEEP READING--YOU HAVEN'T DECIDED WHAT THE ANSWER IS!

ANSWER

Her attention was at least partially contingent upon undesirable behavior.

EXPLANATION:

To induce Heathcliff to remain in his seat more,
Ms. Dimples should attend to him periodically while he is
seated. However, the way that she now seems to be dealing
with the problem is by making reinforcement contingent upon
his getting out of his seat. Apparently the only time that
he is attended to is immediately after he has wandered
around.

IN THE FOLLOWING INCIDENT, IDENTIFY HOW YOU WOULD USE THE
METHOD OF REINFORCEMENT OF INCOMPATIBLE BEHAVIOR TO REDUCE
THE FREQUENCY OF TARDINESS.

Like most of the teachers in your school you have
pupils who are late to class almost every day. You have
tried begging, threatening, screaming, keeping them in after
school, and letters to parents, but the lateness and excuses
persist.

Before you look at the answer, write down the incompatible behavior which you would reinforce, and at least three ways that you might reinforce this behavior.

ANSWER

Obviously, coming on time or coming early is incompatible with tardiness. But you didn't need this book to see that. The question in this case is HOW to reinforce coming in early. Hence -- some ideas:

(1) Organize your class on a point system whereby students earn points for desirable behaviors (e.g., coming to class on time, turning in assignments on time, doing assigned work, writing papers, etc.)

(2) During the first five minutes of every class give a short, easy test over the previous day's work. Give extra credit for correct answers on this quiz.

(3) When one of your chronic "lates" comes in on time, make a point of thanking him (without sarcasm) for making it on time. If you feel that saying it in front of the class wouldn't be wise, whisper it to him. Even a nod or a smile could be reinforcing. You should notice students when they come in on time and should make a conscious effort to let them know that you appreciate it.

(4) If all else fails check: (a) your mouthwash, (b) your deodorant, (c) your toothpaste (maybe you need a whitener), (d) your denture adhesive (maybe the students don't like you because you can't bite into apples), (e) your bleach (are you using an old-fashioned one), (f) your shampoo (maybe what you have isn't ordinary dandruff), (g) your bra (if applicable -- can you cross your heart?), (h) your after-shave and (or) perfume (you can't really tell any more).

Bill is one of thirty students in your fourth grade
class this year. School has only been in session for three
weeks, but he has already missed five days. Though his
mother writes notes to the effect that he was sick on those
days, the other children tell you that she doesn't really
care and that Bill just wanders over the neighborhood when
he doesn't come to school. Even when he is present he takes
little interest in his work, doing only what he has to do
to get by.

What incompatible behavior(s) would you reinforce? _____

_____

NOTE: A student who isn't reinforced for anything that he
does at school just isn't going to like the place. If he
views the classroom as a place where he is humiliated for
not knowing answers, punished for being bored, and never
told anything nice, it is no wonder that he tries to get
away from it every chance that he has. Kids like Bill might
have bad enough problems at home to merit the attention of
the guidance counselor or social workers, but the focus of
the teacher's attention is on the student's school environment. She may not be able to make the student's home life
reinforcing, but she can provide reinforcement for success
and effort in her own classroom.

Thus, if you do not want Bill to stay out of school, then
reinforce him for coming to school.

Before going any further, write the five rules for using
reinforcers and briefly describe how each of these rules
would be used to shape Bill's behavior of coming to school.

ANSWER

REINFORCE SMALL STEPS AT FIRST.

At first you would reinforce him for just coming to
school. The most direct way to go about this would be to
tell him, "I am glad that you are here", "I appreciate your
coming today", or "It is good to see you back." You could
also make school a more positive experience by letting him
know that you notice and appreciate any improvements in his
work. When you see him working, walk by his desk, pat him
on the back, and say something positive about his work. You
could tell him that it makes you feel good to see him there.
If he attempts to answer questions or enter into class dis-
cussions, try to overlook the wrong answers and give him
credit for making some attempt. If you can't remember at
least four comments which would likely reinforce a student
for attempting to answer a question, you should review the
unit on positive reinforcement. You will need to know some
of these responses for the post-test.

GIVE FREQUENT REINFORCEMENT TO ESTABLISH A BEHAVIOR AND
INTERMITTENT REINFORCEMENT TO MAINTAIN IT.

At first you could say something to him every day
when he comes in, but as he begins to come more often
(hopefully) you might make some comment only every second,
third, or fourth day.

MAKE YOUR REINFORCEMENT CONTINGENT ON THE DESIRED BEHAVIOR.

You want to make school reinforcing for Bill, but that
doesn't mean that you have to reinforce everything that he
does at school. You should make every effort to catch him
being good and to provide reinforcement only at those times.
Tell him that you are glad that he has come back to school
BEFORE he has time to get into trouble.

GIVE YOUR REINFORCEMENT IMMEDIATELY AFTER THE DESIRED
BEHAVIOR.

If you can, say something to him when he comes into
the room. Unfortunately, it is often hard to be reinforcing
when the Bills of the world come storming into the classroom.

BE CONSISTENT

Make some positive comment to Bill even on those days when you are in a poor mood.

POST-TEST OVER REINFORCEMENT OF BEHAVIOR
WHICH IS INCOMPATIBLE WITH THE UNDESIRED BEHAVIOR

1. What are three examples of student behaviors which could be dealt with by reinforcement of incompatible behaviors?
   (a)
   (b)
   (c)

2. Susan isn't really a poor student. She occasionally gets into trouble, but in the main poses no real problem. She just seems to be, well, an unenthusiastic scholar.

   What are at least three incompatible behaviors which you could reinforce in attempting to modify Susan's behavior of daydreaming or just staring into space during class?
   (a)
   (b)
   (c)

3. Write the five rules for using reinforcers and under each one tell how that particular rule would be applied to induce Susan to daydream less.
   (a)

   (b)

   (c)

   (d)

   (e)

4. Define incompatible behaviors.

5. Under what circumstances should you use reinforcement of incompatible behavior?

6. Write the four rules for weakening undesirable behaviors.
   (a)
   (b)
   (c)
   (d)

7. Write at least four comments which would positively reinforce a student for attempting to answer a question, even though he has given an incorrect answer.
   (a)
   (b)
   (c)
   (d)

TECHNIQUE II: EXTINCTION

OBJECTIVES:

(1) You will be able to define extinction, stating that it is the process by which behaviors are eliminated by the withdrawal of reinforcement.

(2) You will be able to tell under what circumstances you should use extinction to weaken undesired behaviors.

(3) You will be able to give three examples of student behaviors which could be dealt with by the technique of extinction.

(4) You will be able to write two ways in which teachers maintain undesirable behaviors. These are:
(a) Direct teacher attention
(b) Teacher reactions to student behaviors which lead to reinforcement by peers

(5) You will be able to provide two examples for each of the two ways in which teachers maintain undesirable behavior.

(6) You will be able to tell how to discriminate between behaviors which are maintained by the teacher and behaviors which are maintained by direct peer reinforcement.

(7) Given a classroom situation in which a teacher is attempting to modify a student's behavior by extinction, you will be able to point out errors in the teacher's application of this concept. The errors could be either:
(a) Breaking one or more of the four rules for weakening undesirable behaviors
(b) Breaking one or more of the five rules for using reinforcers
(c) Misinterpreting a temporary increase in undesirable behavior as a failure of the technique of extinction
(d) Misinterpreting a temporary regression in appropriate behavior as a failure of the technique of extinction

50

(e) Failing to distinguish between behavior which is maintained by the teacher and behavior which is maintained by other sources

(8) Given a classroom situation in which one or more students are exhibiting undesirable behavior, you will be able to write how to use extinction to effect some desired change in the students' behavior.

WHAT IS EXTINCTION?

(1) By definition, those behaviors which are reinforced are _____ and those which are not reinforced are _____.

*strengthened
weakened, extinguished

(2) Extinction is the process by which behaviors are eliminated by the withdrawal of reinforcement. If teacher attention maintains a behavior, the withdrawal of this attention probably (will, will not) _____ weaken the behavior.

*will

(3) If direct peer attention reinforces a behavior the withdrawal of teacher attention probably (will, will not) _____ weaken the behavior.

*will not

(4) However, since the teacher is probably the most powerful reinforcer in the classroom, her failure to attend to behavior often causes the behavior to _____.

*weaken, extinguish

(5) When a student raises his hand, the teacher _____ the student by calling on him.

*reinforces

(6) If the teacher called on this student each time that he raised his hand, we would expect the hand raising behavior to _____.

*increase

(7) But if the student raised his hand many times and the teacher never called on him, we would expect the hand raising behavior to _____.

*decrease, weaken

(8) Thus, by not _____ the hand raising the teacher has extinguished this behavior.

*reinforcing or attending to

(9) It is unfortunate that the principle of extinction is often misused in the classroom. There is a tendency for a teacher to ignore those students who do acceptable work and to spend a disproportionate amount of time attempting to control students who behave disruptively and do poor work. In this type of situation the easiest way for the student to obtain attention is to be disruptive or to do exceptionally bad work. In other words, the teacher unknowingly uses extinction to extinguish _____ and positively reinforces _____ with her attention.

*desired behavior
undesired behavior

(10) One of the most common misconceptions in teaching is that the teacher should not let any misbehavior occur without attempting to show her disapproval with a frown, harsh words, trip to the office, etc. However, we have already noted in previous units that ANY FORM OF TEACHER ATTENTION can be reinforcing. Therefore, the teacher can withdraw reinforcement for many undesirable behaviors by _____.

*not attending to them, ignoring them

(11) If she makes a point of positively reinforcing desired behavior at the same time that she is ignoring undesired behavior, we would expect the student to begin making the _____ responses.

*correct, desired

(12) Teachers maintain undesirable student behaviors either by direct teacher attention or by teacher reactions which lead to reinforcement by peers. Direct teacher attention is the "Johnny, stop wandering around, stop

doing this, stop doing that, stop, stop, stop...." type
of reinforcement in which the kid probably gets more
attention than he has ever had in his life - and loves
it. Thus, undesirable behaviors can be maintained by
direct teacher attention if the teacher's attention is
contingent upon _____.

*undesirable behavior

(13) Another way in which inappropriate behavior is reinforced is when that behavior elicits a teacher reaction
which results in peer attention for the offending
student. For example, Johnny puts a tack in the
teacher's chair. The teacher then sits down and either
(a) jumps up with a pained expression on his face,
threatening divine retribution upon the whole class
unless the culprit is turned in, or (b) jerks a little,
unobtrusively grits his teeth and continues with the
lesson, never letting the students know that he is both
hurt and angry. Would the incident be more likely to
be repeated if the teacher acted out alternative a or
alternative b? _____

Why? _____
_____

*a
Alternative a is enormously reinforcing to most
students whereas alternative b is disappointing to
everyone in the class.

(14) If a student regularly cracks his knuckles in spite of
the teacher's repeated admonitions concerning his ill
manners, lack of concern for others, and generally
filthy personal habits, would this knuckle cracking
behavior be more likely to be maintained by direct
teacher attention or by teacher reactions which lead
to reinforcement by peers? _____

*direct teacher attention

(15) If a student loudly scrapes his feet across the fifty-
year-old floor of your classroom until you just can't
stand it any longer and scream "Stop that" (much to the
joy of everyone), in what way would your behavior
probably contribute to the recurrence of the student's
behavior? _____
_____

53

*your reaction would probably elicit peer attention
which would be reinforcing to the student

(16) Regardless of the way in which a behavior has been
maintained by the teacher, she can weaken that behavior by not attending to it. Without her _____
the behavior will also be less likely to be reinforced
by other students.

*attention

(17) Thus she should be able to extinguish both knuckle
cracking and foot scraping by _____.

*ignoring them

(18) As soon as the students realize that reinforcement for
a behavior has been withdrawn, there will be a temporary increase in the frequency of the response. If the
increase is not reinforced, the behavior will gradually
fade out. Thus, once you have withdrawn reinforcement,
the response (should, should not) _____be
reinforced again under any circumstances, especially
during _____.

*should not
the temporary increase in frequency

(19) Likewise, if there is a temporary regression during
extinction (everything goes great for two weeks and
then the little monster starts doing it again), you
should avoid _____.

*reinforcing the behavior

WHEN SHOULD YOU USE EXTINCTION?

(1) Students often refuse to do work because they realize
that their refusal always makes the teacher visibly
irritated. We could weaken this behavior of refusing
to do work by _____
_____.

*not making it a big event, by not giving more atten-
tion for a student's refusal than for his work

(2) However, some behaviors are not maintained by the teacher. Often direct peer attention _____ the behavior regardless of the presence or absence of a teacher response.

*reinforces, maintains

(3) If the undesirable behavior is directly _____ by peer attention, then it will not be _____ if the teacher withholds her attention.

*maintained, reinforced
 extinguished

(4) Therefore, the teacher must discriminate between those undesirable behaviors which are teacher maintained and those which are _____ by other reinforcers.

*maintained

(5) Since no one likes to feel that his behavior maintains undesirable pupil responses, this discrimination is often painfully difficult to make. The only way to make it is for the teacher to change her behavior and observe the effect which this has upon student _____.

*behavior

(6) Thus, if you feel that the reason Susan is yawning so much is that she knows that it infuriates you (bear in mind that there are other reasons for yawning in class), you might withdraw the suspected reinforcement by _____ to see if this has any effect on her behavior.

*not visibly manifesting your irritation

(7) Occasionally, one or two students exhibit behaviors which cannot be ignored because they either disrupt the whole class or present safety hazards. Which of the following behaviors cannot be ignored by the teacher?
(a) Throwing a baseball in the classroom
(b) Daydreaming
(c) Blowing bubbles with bubblegum
(d) Flying a paper airplane

*a and possibly d

55

Ignoring is probably not the best strategy for dealing with <u>all</u> bad behaviors.

(8) You probably cannot _____ fighting in the hall,
but you _____ a student who is tapping a
pencil on his desk.

    *ignore
    can ignore

(9) Thus, extinction is appropriate for most of those
behaviors for which the teacher controls _____,
and for those behaviors in which one or two students do
not disrupt _____ or present _____
_____.

    *the reinforcement
    the whole class
    safety hazards or risks

EXTINCTION AND THE CONFRONTATION GAME:

There are a number of inappropriate student behaviors
which involve confrontations with the teacher. For example,
arguing, cursing, refusing to do work, refusing to comply
with instructions, and "smart talk." Confrontative situations are sufficiently diverse that they can't all be dealt
with by a single technique. There is quite a bit of
difference between little Anne's arguing about the answers
to some test questions (possibly with justification) and an
eighteen year old's wielding a knife. However, the technique of extinction is one of the more useful procedures for
dealing with confrontations.

(1) Oppositional students often take loud, adamant, and
profane positions against the teacher, with the expec-
tation that the teacher will put on a rather good show
of teeth gnashing, grimacing, yelling, threatening,
issuing more orders, and in general, acting acutely
frustrated. To utilize extinction you would withdraw
reinforcement by _____
_____.

    *not exhibiting any of these behaviors, keeping your
        cool, letting the student do all of the raving and
        blustering.

(2) Then, if you feel that the student's behavior is
serious enough, you can use extinction in combination
with some other method of weakening behavior. This
would involve a clear statement of the inappropriate

behavior and the consequences, while avoiding the
arguments and emotional reactions which would be
_____ to the students.

*reinforcing

(3) Thus, extinction does not always involve completely
     ignoring the student's inappropriate behavior. If a
     student stands up cursing and arguing with you,
     response cost, time-out, or some form of punishment can
     be imposed on him while at the same time you can imple-
     ment extinction by _____
     _____
     _____.

*not arguing, acting frustrated etc.; possibly even
     ignoring him until he has calmed down; letting him
     stand up there and argue and curse by himself

(4) On the other hand, less noxious forms of argument could
     be dealt with effectively with only the technique of
     _____.

*extinction

THINK ABOUT THE FOLLOWING INCIDENT IN TERMS OF WHAT YOU HAVE
LEARNED ABOUT EXTINCTION.

     Mr. Matthews has a student, James W., in his 8th grade
English class who constantly asks questions which have
absolutely nothing to do with the daily lessons. Since
these interruptions distract the class, Mr. Matthews has
made a point of scolding James, often becoming visibly irritated in the process. Making James stay after school quietens him for a few days, but he is soon asking irrelevant
questions again. After talking the problem over with the
guidance counselor, Mr. Matthews decided to try ignoring
these disruptions. In other words, he decided to try the
technique of extinction. Mr. Matthews was very consistent
in ignoring James' distractive behavior. He made a mental
note never to answer any question asked by James. Though
at first James asked more than his usual number of irrelevant questions, he gradually asked fewer and fewer. But
Mr. Matthews was adamant--he never once paid any attention
to James. However, though James does not ask as many
irrelevant questions as before, he is still a nuisance. He

58

has even begun to drop his books on the floor rather often and taps his pencil on the desk constantly.

WHICH OF THE FOLLOWING ERRORS DID MR. MATTHEWS MAKE IN APPLYING THE CONCEPT OF EXTINCTION?
(Choose one or more of the following; answers are below)

(a)   Mr. Matthews was inconsistent in ignoring the undesired behavior.

(b)   Since Mr. Matthews had not previously reinforced the undesired behavior, he should not have expected ignoring it to be effective.

(c)   Behaviors reinforced concurrently with nonreinforced contraproductive behaviors have little linear continuity with their temporal equivalents--more or less.

(d)   Mr. Matthews failed to positively reinforce desired behavior while he was ignoring the undesired behavior.

ANSWER

d

EXPLANATION

(a)   He was consistent.

(b)   James was probably reinforced by the attention from his teacher. This was especially evident when the ignoring of all of James' behavior resulted in a partial extinction of the questioning behavior and an attempt to gain attention in new ways.

(c)   Huh?

(d)   Mr. Matthews should have reinforced James when he asked relevant questions. The idea is not to totally ignore a student, but to only ignore him when he is emitting inappropriate behaviors. If relevant questions had been reinforced, James would have gotten the attention (which he seems to find so rewarding) in an acceptable manner. However, he was shut off from contact with the teacher and given no alternative way to earn recognition. So we find him seeking it in other ways, e.g., dropping his books and tapping his pencil.

FOR THE FOLLOWING INCIDENT, IDENTIFY HOW YOU WOULD USE THE PRINCIPLES OF EXTINCTION TO INDUCE SANDRA TO ONLY RAISE HER HAND WHEN SHE WANTS TO BE CALLED ON.

When you ask a question in class, Sandra will not sit still if she knows the answer. She waves her hands, half-stands in her desk, and yells, "I know, I know!" Though you want to call on any student who can answer your questions, you do not want your students yelling, waving their hands, and getting out of their seats.

Before reading our answer, write down how you would utilize extinction to deal with this situation. Include a list of the five rules for using reinforcers and a brief description of the way in which each of these rules would be applied.

ANSWER

(1) Ignore her each time that she emits the undesirable behaviors (waving her hands, yelling, and raising up in her seat).

(2) Positively reinforce her when she emits the desired behavior:

(a) Reinforce small steps at first--If Sandra never just raises her hand, the first step might be to give her positive reinforcement (e.g., asking her for the answer when she does not yell at you). After she has stopped yelling, you might reinforce her only when she neither yells nor raises up in her seat. The next step (after she consistently neither yells nor raises up) would be to call upon her when she only raises her hand.

(b) Give frequent reinforcement to establish a behavior and intermittent reinforcement to maintain it--At first, call on Sandra each time that she emits the desired behavior. After she has learned that you will only call on her when she raises her hand, you will need to give her

60

intermittent reinforcement (just as you will be giving all other students who emit desired behaviors). In other words, you must still positively reinforce good work, but not every time that it occurs.

(c) Make your reinforcement contingent on the desired behavior--Call on her ONLY when she makes the desired response. If you slip and call on her when she is yelling, it will take much longer to extinguish this behavior.

(d) Give your reinforcement immediately after the desired behavior--As soon as she quietly raises her hand, call on her. Don't wait until next Monday to tell her that you appreciated it.

(e) Be consistent--Positively reinforce what you set out to reinforce. Do not reinforce her raising her hand one day and her yelling the next. If you are inconsistent the student has no way of knowing what you really want. Regardless of what you say you want, students look at what you do.

POST-TEST OVER EXTINCTION

1. Define extinction.

2. Mr. Jones has been having trouble all year with Sally's habit of arguing with practically everything that he says. At first Mr. Jones always tried to reason with her, but he soon gave this tactic up. Now he either tells her to be quiet or just gives her a fierce look to let her know that he disapproves of this "smart talk."

   In terms of what you have learned of reinforcement, what is one explanation for Susan's arguing (besides the idea that Mr. Jones might always be wrong)?

3. How would you use the concepts of extinction and reinforcement of incompatible behaviors to eliminate Susan's arguing with Mr. Jones?

61

(a) Reinforcement of incompatible behaviors:

(b) Extinction:

4. Give three examples of student behaviors which could be dealt with by the technique of extinction.
   (a)
   (b)
   (c)

5. Write the four rules for weakening undesirable behavior.
   (a)

   (b)

   (c)

   (d)

6. Write two ways in which teachers often maintain undesirable behaviors.
   (a)
   (b)

7. Give two examples of each of the ways in which teachers often maintain undesirable behaviors.
   (a)
   (b)

   (a)
   (b)

8. Ms. Winston teaches 7th grade in what the school board politely chooses to call a "traditional school building" (the teachers refer to it as a dilapidated fire trap). Because of the wooden floors, the slightest movement of a desk makes a loud scraping-creaking or creaking-scraping noise. Since the students have found that this noise bothers Ms. Winston to no end, it has become a game in her classes to see who can irritate her the

most without getting caught. Though she tries to
punish the guilty students, it is difficult to tell
who has moved their desk the slight amount required
to make the noise. The school psychologist advised her
to just ignore the disruptions and hope that they go
away. Though skeptical of letting anyone get away with
such behavior (and skeptical of anything that the
school psychologist says), she agreed to try. However,
as soon as the students got the idea that no one was
going to have to stay after school for this sin, the
room became a cacophony of creaking and scraping, much
to the amusement of everyone (except possibly Ms. Winston). By the last period, she was so incensed that she
sent three pupils to the office, gave everyone else a
lecture on their lack of manners, and vowed never again
to ignore anything--"for everyone just goes wild."

Ms. Winston has obviously made a number of mistakes in
dealing with these students.
Which of the following errors did Ms. Winston make in
applying the concept of extinction?

(a) Breaking one of the four rules for weakening
     undesired behavior
(b) Breaking one or more of the five rules of using
     reinforcement
(c) Misinterpreting a temporary increase in undesir-
     able behavior as a failure of the technique
     of extinction
(d) Failing to distinguish between the behavior which
     is maintained by the teacher and the behavior which
     is reinforced by other sources

9. How would you utilize the concept of extinction to
    eliminate the desk-scraping in Ms. Winston's class?

10. How do you discriminate between behaviors which are
     maintained by the teacher and behaviors which are
     maintained by direct peer reinforcement?

11. Under what circumstances should you use extinction to weaken undesired behavior?

12. How do you utilize extinction, either by itself or in combination with some other technique, to deal with student-teacher confrontations?

TECHNIQUE III: TIME-OUT

OBJECTIVES:

(1)   You will be able to define time-out, stating that it is
      the process by which behaviors are eliminated by remov-
      ing the student from the source of reinforcement.

(2)   You will be able to tell under what circumstances you
      should use time-out to weaken undesirable behavior.

(3)   You will be able to give three examples of student
      behaviors which could be dealt with by the technique
      of time-out.

(4)   Given a classroom situation in which a teacher is
      attempting to modify a student's behavior by the use of
      time-out, you will be able to point out errors in the
      teacher's application of this concept. The errors
      could be either:
      (a)   Breaking one or more of the five rules of posi-
            tive reinforcement.
      (b)   Breaking one or more of the four rules of weak-
            ening behavior.
      (c)   Providing an inadequate time-out area.
      (d)   Focusing attention on the student being sent to
            time-out.
      (e)   Not having a pre-specified period of time (five or
            ten minutes) for students to remain in the time-
            out area.

(5)   Given a classroom situation in which one or more
      students are exhibiting undesirable behavior, you will
      be able to describe how to use time-out to effect some
      desired change in the students' behavior.

WHAT IS TIME-OUT?

      Some undesirable behaviors are so disruptive or hazard-
ous that it is impossible for you to conduct your class as
long as these behaviors continue. Since the behaviors must
be stopped immediately, the process of extinction is inappropriate. Under these circumstances it may be necessary to
move the offending student away from his peers. Moving the
student to a designated time-out area can be beneficial in
two ways: He is no longer able to disrupt your class and
social reinforcement for his disruptive behavior is no

longer available.

(1) Both extinction and time-out are techniques to keep
     the student from being _____ for undesirable
     behavior.

     *reinforced

(2) In the process of extinction you eliminate the behavior
     by _____.

     *withdrawing the reinforcement from it

(3) In time-out you eliminate the behavior by removing the
     student from the source of reinforcement. Thus, if a
     pupil who is throwing objects is being reinforced with
     peer attention we might use time-out to move the
     student _____. By doing this
     we have removed him from the source of _____.

     *away from his peers
      reinforcement

(4) The classroom should have a specified time-out area.
     This might be a cloak room or a corner of the room
     hemmed in by bookcases or cabinets. If no such area
     exists, the teacher should construct one by rearranging
     furniture in the classroom. Because you wish to remove
     the learner from the source of positive reinforcement
     the time-out area (should, should not) _____
     be interesting.

     *should not

(5) The corner of the room with all of the science equip-
     ment would not be an effective time-out area for a
     student who loves _____.

     *science

(6) The whole idea of time-out is that the classroom situa-
     tion provides more _____ than the time-out
     area.

     *reinforcement

66

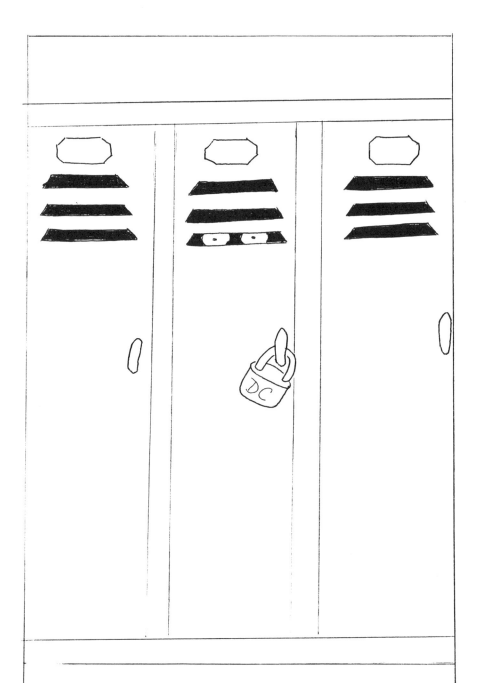

Some rather obvious places <u>don't</u> make good time-out areas.

(7) Therefore, you (would, would not) _____
send a student who hated spelling into the time-out
area during spelling lessons.

*would not

(8) But time-out would be effective if you sent a student
who enjoyed spelling into the time-out area during
_____ lessons.

*spelling

(9) A student who enjoys peer attention probably (will,
will not) _____ be reinforced by sitting
by himself in the time-out area.

*will not

(10) You do not chastise a student when he is sent to the
time-out area. The whole process should be as matter-
of-fact as possible. If the student violates certain
rules, he is asked to go to the time-out area. There
should be no lectures, no moralizing, no "see there, I
warned you." The object is to deprive the student of
_____. Therefore you should
focus as little attention as possible on the disrupting student. If you yell or act disgusted, your reaction to the misbehavior might be _____
to the student. Needless to say, it is often
rewarding to frustrate the teacher.

*positive reinforcement
reinforcing

(11) Though most teachers have a Dennis the Menace whom
they would like to send to time-out forever, you need
to let the whole class know that there is a set period
of time for anyone to remain in the time-out area.
Usually five minutes is long enough. For instance, if
you say "John, go to the time-out area," the student
knows that he must stay there for _____ minutes.

*five

(12) An exception to the idea of having a set period of
time for a child to remain in time-out would be the
case in which the child is screaming or crying during
time-out. Unless you feel that the student is in

68

physical danger, he should not be given any reinforcement for his crying. Thus, he should remain in the time-out area until _____.

*he has stopped crying

(13) At this point you might be asking yourself how you are going to convince a physically mature (big - real big), recalcitrant (mean as hell), high school senior (everyone was afraid to flunk him) to go to the time-out area. We don't really know. The difficulty of getting some older students to actually leave their seats and go to the time-out area could make this technique impossible to implement. In elementary school, especially at the primary level, this is not a problem. However, we might expect this method to have less application in _____
_____
_____.

*high schools and junior high schools, especially in areas with a high rate of delinquency.

WHEN SHOULD YOU USE TIME-OUT?

(1) If your reactions are maintaining undesirable student behavior, ignoring the undesirable behavior will probably extinguish it. However, if the student is acting out for the direct attention of his peers, _____ would be more effective.

*time-out

(2) Thus, time-out is an excellent technique to use with those behaviors which are directly maintained by _____ or those behaviors which are so disruptive or hazardous that _____ as long as they continue. Behaviors which are not disruptive of the whole class or which are maintained by teacher attention should be dealt with by the technique of _____.

*peer attention
 you can't conduct class
 extinction

69

There are some circumstances which can make time-out
difficult to implement.

(3) For which of the following behaviors should time-out
     be used?
     (a) pushing and shoving during free time
     (b) students coming to your desk to ask questions
          when they should raise their hands
     (c) daydreaming
     (d) someone disrupting those around him with jokes

     *a,d

THINK ABOUT THE FOLLOWING INCIDENT IN TERMS OF WHAT YOU HAVE
LEARNED ABOUT TIME-OUT

   Seymore is Ms. Anderson's self-appointed class jester.
Hardly a day goes by that he does not throw the whole class
into fits of laughter. Even Ms. Anderson has to admit that
the kid is hilarious. Nevertheless, it is almost impossible
to carry on any type of class discussion or even a lecture
without Seymore's disrupting the whole affair. At first
Ms. Anderson attempted to punish Seymore with verbal reprimands and by sending him to the office. However, neither
seemed to work, and she really hated to be too severe with a
child with so great a gift for making others laugh. Then
she tried to extinguish the disruptive behavior by ignoring
it, but it seemed that Seymore couldn't care less whether
the teacher appreciated him or not. Finally, Ms. Anderson
decided to move Seymore away from his peers every time that
he made a disruptive remark or gesture, i.e., she decided to
remove him from the source of reinforcement. So she began
sending him from his seat (directly in front of her desk) to
the back of the room to stand in the corner for five minutes every time that he engaged in his disruptive levity.
However, this arrangement didn't seem to be very effective.
The other students were constantly turning around to see
what Seymore was doing, and each time that she told him to
go to the rear of the room, everyone went into stitches
just watching him saunter back there.

WHICH OF THE FOLLOWING ERRORS DID MS. ANDERSON MAKE IN
APPLYING THE CONCEPT OF TIME-OUT?
(Choose one or more of the following; answers are on next
 page)

(a) Ms. Anderson obviously wasn't consistent in removing
     Seymore from his peers.
(b) The corner of the room isn't a good time-out area.
(c) Ms. Anderson focused attention on Seymore when she sent

71

him to the rear of the room

(d) Time-out isn't "strong enough" to deal with disruptions on this scale.

(e) Ms. Anderson probably had halitosis.

ANSWER

b,c

EXPLANATION

(a) She probably was consistent, especially if she did send him back every time he exhibited his disruptive behavior.

(b) It is best to keep the student in time-out completely hidden from his classmates. This is particularly important for someone with Seymore's talents. To stand him up where everyone can see him is like putting him on stage.

(c) Even though she apparently was careful not to yell, jump up and down, shout obscentities, and throw erasers at poor defenseless Seymore, Ms. Anderson unwittingly focused attention on him by the arrangement of his desk with respect to the time-out area. With a desk in front of the room, Seymore had to walk the length of the class to get to the corner. This arrangement left plenty of time (while his back was to the teacher) to make faces and be the center of attention. Thus, Seymore was again put on stage.

(d) Humbug

(e) Now really -- is that relevant?

FOR THE FOLLOWING INCIDENT, IDENTIFY HOW YOU WOULD USE TIME-OUT TO INDUCE TOM TO TALK LESS WHEN HE SHOULD BE WORKING.

Tom, a student in your 5th grade, is a "talker." He never seems to run out of something to say. At the first of the year he and two other boys sat in the rear of the room and talked constantly. It did not take long for you to realize that they had to be separated. After they were placed in different parts of the room the other two quieted down, but the switch didn't seem to faze Tom. You have tried to ignore him when he just chatters and to reinforce him when he asks questions on lesson material or contributes to a class discussion, but it is evident that Tom thrives more on the attention which his fellow students give to his running commentaries on football, baseball, etc., than he does on your approval.

Write down how you would utilize time-out in this situation, specifying what you would tell Tom and what behaviors you would positively reinforce.

ANSWER

(1) Tell Tom that from now on, any time that he talks to anyone during the time when he should be working, he will be sent to the time-out area for five minutes. The next time that he talks, do it! Don't give him warnings or make threats -- just do it! Also, don't preach sermons, tell the class that you are making an example of him, or make an issue out of the incident. Your purpose is not to focus attention on Tom.

(2) Positively reinforce Tom when he makes desirable responses (participates in a class discussion, volunteers to answer questions, gives book reports). All of these activities are desirable ways of gaining attention.

POST-TEST OVER TIME-OUT

1. To Ms. Burns' chagrin, her fifth graders have recently made the transition from the "obnoxious noises" stage of pre-adolescent development to the "paper wad" stage. Furious at this latest onslaught against classroom tranquility, she has decided to "nip it in the bud." Each time students are caught shooting paper wads, she sends everyone involved into the cloak room for five minutes. For those students who don't seem impressed with this procedure, their trip to the cloak room is accompanied by a few sharp words on the upbringing of anyone with the audacity to disobey her.

In terms of what you know of time-out which of the following error(s) is Ms. Burns making?

(a) She is not immediate in her response.

(b) She is not "matter-of-fact" in sending students to time-out.

(c) The time-out area that she has arranged probably isn't dull.

(d) She is focusing attention on students sent to time-out.

2. Define time-out.

3. Under what circumstances should you use time-out to weaken undesired behavior?

4. What are three examples of student behaviors which should be dealt with by the technique of time-out?

(a)

(b)

(c)

5. John is one of those students who really has a hard time sitting still. He often gets up and wanders around the room when everyone is supposed to be working on individual assignments. Not only does this hinder his own work, but talking and joking with other pupils makes it difficult for them to complete their assignments.

How would you use time-out and reinforcement of incompatible behavior to keep John from wandering around the room so much?

6. For three weeks Ms. Henderson attempted to eliminate disruptive behaviors in her first grade through the use of time-out. For one or two days it seemed to be working, but the effect soon wore off and the kids were just as rowdy as ever. Complaining to the school counselor, Ms. Henderson said that she had been consistent in sending the disruptive pupils to time-out every time that they misbehaved. She has provided an isolated time-out area, utilizing a large cardboard refrigerator packing crate which she had secured from the dining room. She had taken care to explain to everyone that when they were disruptive they would have to spend five minutes in the box, and that the box was a very evil place. Moreover, she had made a special effort to be more positively reinforcing to the students when they exhibited appropriate behaviors.

In spite of Ms. Henderson's otherwise conscientious use of the technique of time-out, she has still provided an inadequate time-out area. What, exactly, is wrong with the time-out area which she has utilized?

7. Every class seems to have a tattletale in it. To your dismay, your sixth grade seems to have more than its quota. What is the single most appropriate technique (reinforcement of incompatible behaviors, extinction, or time-out) for dealing with this problem?

How would you utilize this technique in dealing with tattletaling?

TECHNIQUE IV: RESPONSE COST

OBJECTIVES:

(1) You will be able to define response cost, stating that
     it is a procedure in which the student systematically
     loses positive reinforcers when he behaves inappro-
     priately.

(2) You will be able to tell under what circumstances you
     should use response cost to weaken undesirable behavior.

(3) You will be able to give three examples of student
     behaviors which could be dealt with by the technique
     of response cost.

(4) You will be able to give three variations of response
     cost which might be applied in the classroom. These
     are:
     (a) Giving the students the opportunity to earn rein-
          forcers for emitting appropriate behavior, but
          systematically deducting reinforcers when
          inappropriate behavior is emitted.
     (b) Making new reinforcers available (the student
          doesn't have to earn them) but systematically
          reducing the student's access to these rein-
          forcers when he emits an inappropriate behavior.
     (c) Removing an existing privilege if the student
          emits a specific inappropriate behavior.

(5) You will be able to give an example of each of these
     three types of response cost.

(6) You will be able to tell what the differences are
     between individual and group contingencies in terms
     of:
     (a) Who is fined for inappropriate behavior.
     (b) Logistics.

(7) You will be able to give two reasons why group contin-
     gencies might be employed in a classroom.

(8) You will be able to tell two ways to prevent a student
     from losing more reinforcers than are available to him.

(9) Given a classroom situation in which a teacher is
     attempting to modify a student's behavior by the use of

response cost, you will be able to point out errors in the teacher's application of this concept. The errors will involve:

(a) Breaking one or more of the four rules of weakening behavior

(b) Breaking one or more of the five rules of positive reinforcement

(c) Using an excessive fine

(d) Not placing some limit on the number of reinforcers which can be lost during a set period of time

(e) Using back-up rewards which have minimal reinforcement value

(f) Not systematically applying the contingencies

(10) Given a classroom situation in which one or more students are exhibiting undesirable behavior, you will be able to describe how to use response cost to effect some desired change in the students' behavior.

WHAT IS RESPONSE COST?

(1) Response cost is a procedure in which the student <u>systematically</u> <u>loses</u> <u>positive</u> <u>reinforcers</u> when he behaves inappropriately. You might view response cost as a fine. The student is rewarded for desirable behaviors but he is _____ for inappropriate behaviors.

*fined

(2) Extinction, time-out, and response cost are similar in that all three techniques make inappropriate behaviors less reinforcing. Extinction withholds reinforcement for behaviors, time-out removes _____ _____, and response cost systematically _____ for inappropriate behaviors.

*the student from the source of reinforcement
 subtracts positive reinforcement

(3) If response cost is used with some system of earning points, privileges, tokens, or tangibles, the student accumulates these positive reinforcers for emitting specific _____ behaviors but loses them if he emits certain specific _____ behaviors.

77

At least, we can endorse the spirit of his explanation.

*appropriate
inappropriate

(4) In other words, the student loses some of the reinforcers which he has _____.

*been working to earn

(5) One way (hopefully out of many) that you might utilize
this to induce your fourth graders to study their
spelling words is to give them one minute of free time
for each word spelled correctly on your daily spelling
quiz. But another rule might be that anyone caught
cheating would lose a specified amount of free time.
In this case the response of _____
would cost a student _____.

*cheating
some of his free time

(6) Another form of response cost is to make reinforcers
available, but to systmatically reduce the student's
access to these reinforcers each time that he emits
a disruptive behavior. For example, "From now on, you
will be given fifteen minutes of free time at the end
of each class period if you exhibit no disruptive
behavior during that class. However, for each instance
of disruptive behavior, you will lose one minute of
_____.

*your free time

(7) Thus, two ways which you might utilize response cost
are to give the student an opportunity to _____
by emitting appropriate behaviors, but to systematically deduct from the reinforcers which he has earned
when he emits inappropriate behaviors, and to _____
_____ but systematically reduce the
student's access to these reinforcers each time that he
emits an inappropriate behavior.

*earn reinforcers
make reinforcers available

(8) A more impromptu use of response cost is simply to
tell a student that if he exhibits a certain behavior
he will lose a specific existing reinforcer. For example, to "Who's gonna make me?" the teacher might

reply "No one will <u>make</u> you do anything, but if you don't return to your seat you will not go to basketball practice this afternoon." In this case the teacher is letting the student know that a specific inappropriate behavior will result in _____

_____.

*the loss of an existing privilege or reinforcer

(9) In all three of the examples the teacher has stated the contingencies ("If you do . . ., then you will be fined . . .") which tells the student what the _____ of emitting specific inappropriate behaviors are.

*consequences

(10) The number of reinforcers lost and the types of behaviors for which the student loses these reinforcers should be explicitly understood. The student is put in the position of making a choice between specific alternatives. He can do certain things and be reinforced, or he can make other types of responses and _____.

*lose specified reinforcers

(11) Response cost can be administered either on an individual or a group contingency basis. When it is utilized with individuals, each student is fined for inappropriate behaviors which he emits. When it is applied as a group contingency the _____ is fined for infractions of the rules by any of its members.

*whole group

(12) Group contingent response cost seems to be one of the most effective techniques for reducing disruptive behaviors of a large number of students. It can be applied to the class as a whole or groups within the class. Group contingencies might aid a teacher in regaining control of a classroom that has gotten out of hand, serve as a transition phase from chaos to individual contingencies, or in the form of team competition, serve as a change of pace for everyone. Though you might not like the idea of permanently organizing your class on the basis of group contingencies, this

80

method might be justified in _____
classrooms or as _____.

*very disruptive, chaotic
a change of pace

(13) At any rate, the logistics of group contingencies are
minimal. The teacher establishes a reinforcer for the
group, makes the contingencies clear, and then
systematically _____ from this reinforcement
whenever pre-specified undesirable behaviors are
exhibited.

*deducts

(14) To provide fifteen minutes of free time if no disruptions occur, the teacher might write a large "15" on
the board. Then, when she observes an infraction of
the rules she would erase the 15 and write 14, signi-
fying that _____
_____.

*only fourteen minutes of free time were then available

(15) Surprisingly enough, students who are already taking
fifty minutes of illegal "free time" will usually work
to obtain ten or fifteen minutes of teacher sanctioned
free time, especially if (or only if) interesting
books, games, and other activities are provided in
_____ that are not available at
other times.

*free time

(16) Response cost with individual contingencies might be
considered more desirable in the sense that each
student is responsible only for _____.

*his own behavior

(17) However, since the teacher must use some system of
record keeping to know the number of minutes of free
time that each student has lost, when different
students should leave the free time area, etc., the
logistics of individual contingencies make it _____
_____.

*more difficult to implement

81

(18) You will occasionally encounter students who are so
      angry at losing a few reinforcers that they don't care
      how many they might lose. To prevent the student
      from losing far more reinforcers than are available to
      him, you should set some limit on the number which can
      be lost in one day or in one class period. Anyone who
      exhibits enough inappropriate behaviors to lose more
      than this _____ should either be removed from
      the classroom for a pre-specified period of time or
      sent to the time-out area within the classroom. In
      doing this the student is given time to calm down in
      an area which is not reinforcing (e.g., the time-out
      area) and may even be aversive to him (e.g., the
      principal's outer office). In addition, by being
      removed from the classroom activity, the student is
      temporarily denied the privilege of earning _____.

      *limit
       reinforcers

(19) Another way to keep the student from losing more
      reinforcers than he has available is to make some
      compromise between a "cost" which is strong enough to
      discourage the undesirable behavior and yet not so
      strong that the student will be completely demoralized
      after one fine. Therefore, the cost should not be
      _____, and there should be some limit on
      _____.

      *excessive
       the number of tokens which can be lost in one period
       of time

(20) Earlier we gave examples of three variations of
      response cost which you might employ. The first
      variation, in which the student is given the oppor-
      tunity to earn reinforcers, is most appropriate for
      use in conjunction with some system of _____
      _____.

      *earning points, tokens, or tangibles

(21) Probably one of the most effective means of combining
      the concepts of positive reinforcement and response
      cost is a contingency contract system in which the
      teacher utilizes student input to decide what behav-
      iors are appropriate and inappropriate within the
      classroom. Since both students and teachers agree

to work with this arrangement of positive reinforcement and response cost, the system is called a

_____ .

*contract, contingency contract

(22) Any behavior which both students and teachers agree
is desirable classroom behavior can be directly reinforced under a contingency contract. In fact, a
contract should stress a variety of ways in which
reinforcers can be earned. Some of the behaviors
which might earn points or tokens are: Bringing paper
and pencil to class, turning in assignments, and
percentage of correct answers on homework. Some other
possibilities are: _____

_____ .

*coming to class on time, answering lesson-related
    questions, participating in class discussions,
    giving reports

(23) In contrast to the positive reinforcement section of
the contract, the response cost portion should be as
brief as possible. A few broad categories of inappropriate behavior can be identified with specific
examples of behavior which would come under each of
these categories. The intention is not to be vague
but rather to de-emphasize the _____ aspects
of the contract.

*negative

(24) Hence, rather than stating that points will be lost
for coming in late, leaving early, talking too loudly,
hitting, _ad infinitum_, one might indicate that a
certain number of points will be lost for each instance
of class disruption, and then provide several _____
of what would be considered class disruption.

*examples

(25) Points or tokens which are earned under this type of
system could be traded in for backup reinforcement such
as free time, tangible rewards, or special privileges
of any sort. Special privileges such as field trips or
parties, and tangibles such as candy or stars on a
chart are usually most appropriate for _____ level

classrooms. However, free time can be utilized
_____ .

*primary
for both primary and secondary levels

(26) If space is limited (as it is in most secondary
school classrooms) the free time area in the room
might serve only as a place to store puzzles, books,
magazines, or games which the students could pick up
and take to their desks. If the space is available,
though, a separate area in the room might be designated where students who have free time can _____
_____ .

*go to read, play games, primp, talk

(27) Delivery of reinforcement or implementation of cost
should be as rapid as possible. Points and tokens
should be presented _____ .

*immediately

(28) Backup reinforcers should be delivered as soon as
possible, particularly when you are just beginning to
utilize a reinforcement/cost system. Rather than have
extensive free time periods at the end of the week it
would be better to have _____ .

*short, daily periods

(29) If points are used, some record keeping procedure is
necessary. Since students should always be aware of
their point status, the records should be readily
available to them. Therefore, it would be _____
for the teacher to keep the record only in his gradebook.

*inappropriate

(30) Some possible methods of record keeping are: Tally
sheets taped on each pupil's desk and maintained by
either pupil or teacher; wall charts maintained by
either teacher or pupil. Another possibility might be:
_____ .

*individual records in each students' notebook with the
teacher maintaining a master copy

84

Just a typical free time period at the John K. Birch Academy.

(31)   However, if you do not wish to organize a token or
        point system, you must rely on variations of response
        cost in which you either make _____
        _____ or
        simply tell the student that _____
        _____.

        *reinforcers available and systematically reduce
            access to them
         if he exhibits a specific behavior he will lose a
            specific positive reinforcer

(32)   If you are utilizing the form of response cost in
        which reinforcers are made available and access to
        them is systematically reduced, you should make NEW
        reinforcers available rather then utilize privileges
        which students now have. In any case, going to the
        bathroom and going to lunch should not be viewed as
        manipulatable reinforcers. Therefore, you should try
        to make reinforcers available by _____
        _____.

        *adding new activities or privileges to your classroom

(33)   To tell a student that if he doesn't do something he
        will lose some existing privileges is likely to elicit
        some rebellion. Thus, if possible, you should struc-
        ture the response cost contingencies so that you rely
        on the reduction of access to new activities or
        privileges rather than _____
        _____.

        *on the loss of existing privileges

WHEN SHOULD YOU USE RESPONSE COST?

(1)   Since the emphasis of this unit has been on the
        removal of positive reinforcement for inappropriate
        behaviors, it bears repeating that regardless of the
        technique you are utilizing to weaken undesired
        behaviors, you should ALWAYS reinforce _____
        _____.

        *desired behaviors

(2)   However, even with proper use of positive reinforce-
        ment, it is likely that you will encounter behaviors
        which are incompatible with your teaching objectives.

86

When this occurs, response cost and time-out should be
utilized only if _____ and reinforcement
of _____ are not sufficient
to eliminate the behaviors.

*extinction
incompatible behaviors

(3) Since time-out requires that the student be willing
to go to the time-out area when requested to do so,
this procedure is probably more appropriate for
_____, whereas response
cost can be used with _____
_____.

*younger students
older students, students of all ages

(4) In addition, it is difficult to send more than one or
two students to the time-out area simultaneously. If
the teacher is confronted with persistent disruptions
by a large number of students, _____
might be more appropriate.

*response cost

(5) Thus, some factors to consider in determining whether
to use response cost or time-out (or both) to "back-up"
extinction and reinforcement of incompatible behaviors
are the difficulties of _____
_____, the _____ of the
students, and the _____ of disrupting
students.

*putting the student in time-out
age
number

(6) Therefore, response cost is more likely to be appropriate when _____
_____.

*disruptive students are old, recalcitrant, or numerous

(7) One of the advantages of response cost is that the
utilization of this technique avoids many of the
problems associated with confrontative behaviors. If
the student refuses to comply with directions, he is

87

_____.

*fined

(8) If he curses you, it isn't necessary to see that he
     does something or goes somewhere for punishment. To
     avoid reinforcing the behavior you use the technique of
     _____, and to further weaken it you
     use _____.

*extinction
 response cost

THINK ABOUT THE FOLLOWING INCIDENT IN TERMS OF WHAT YOU HAVE
LEARNED ABOUT RESPONSE COST.

     By skillful utilization of time-out and extinction
Mr. Jones had eliminated most of the inappropriate behaviors
in his classroom, but a few students were still giving him
problems. Impressed with the idea of response cost, he
decided to penalize students when they emitted certain
inappropriate behaviors. Realizing that he should provide
the students with some explanation of what was going on, he
took care to tell them that "from now on any time that you
do anything wrong, you will be fined for it." Thus, when
Sandy and Priscilla began talking in class, he told them
that their inappropriate behavior had cost them recess,
and when John came into class late after lunch, he told him
that reporting to class late would cost him the privilege
of going to the library that afternoon.

WHICH OF THE FOLLOWING ERRORS DID MR. JONES MAKE IN APPLYING
THE CONCEPT OF RESPONSE COST?
(Choose one or more of the following; answers are below)

(a) He did not direct his responses at specific student
     behaviors
(b) He did not make the contingencies clear
(c) He did not use a large enough fine
(d) He was not immediate in his response
(e) He did not make new reinforcers available

ANSWERS

b,e

EXPLANATION

(a) In these two examples Mr. Jones did an excellent job
     of telling the students exactly what they had done
     wrong.
(b) The contingencies weren't clear at all. We don't have
     any explanation of what a fine is or what Mr. Jones
     means by "anything wrong." Even if the students have
     a general idea of what Mr. Jones considers inappro-
     priate, they are still going to have to misbehave to
     find out what the consequences are. If every infrac-
     tion of the rules merits the same cost, then he only
     needed to state the types of misbehaviors which
     wouldn't be tolerated and the cost, but if different
     behaviors merited different costs, then the various
     cost contingencies needed to be delineated. The idea
     is to give the student the opportunity to consider,
     in advance, the consequences of his actions.
(c) Actually, the fines seem to be excessive. For example,
     we wonder if Sandy and Priscilla would be motivated
     to work hard the rest of the day after having already
     "blown" recess.
(d) Apparently, his response was rapid.
(e) Taking away privileges which have always been avail-
     able is likely to produce a number of very resentful
     students.

IN THE FOLLOWING INCIDENT, IDENTIFY HOW YOU WOULD WEAKEN THE
UNDESIRABLE BEHAVIORS OF THROWING THINGS, YELLING, RUNNING,
AND FIGHTING BY THE USE OF RESPONSE COST PROCEDURES.

     Ms. Smith has just taken over an eighth grade English
class in an inner city school. Though she knew better than
to expect twenty-five eager young minds grasping for pearls
of wisdom, she wasn't quite prepared for thirty-five
yelling, jumping, running, fighting, cursing "pupils."
Vaguely familiar with behavior modification, she valiantly
embarked upon a campaign of extinction in combination with
reinforcement of incompatible behavior. But alas, there
was precious little desirable behavior to reinforce and the
students didn't really care whether she attended to them or
not. She then tried time-out, but how can you put seventeen
kids into the time-out area at the same time and still keep
it a dull place?

Write how you would utilize an appropriate form of response cost to weaken these behaviors.

Probably the best action that Ms. Smith could take at this point would be to initiate a response cost system with group contingencies, making reinforcers available but systematically reducing the group's access to these reinforcers with each disruptive behavior.

(a) She should not give up on utilizing positive reinforcement. The success of response cost or any other technique of weakening behavior depends to a large extent upon the positive alternatives that are available to the student. Let's face it -- wreaking havoc in a classroom is fun (reinforcing) to many students.

(b) Establish a reinforcer: Since they probably haven't had any experience with the systematic use of free time, you should take care to offer enough free time and enticing enough activities to make them work for it. Offering fifteen minutes of free time during each class period is not an excessive amount to start with. In addition, let them engage in as many activities as you possibly can in your classroom. Allow sleeping, primping, and as much loud talking, radios, records, and games as possible. You are going to have to shape their behavior, even their free time behavior. Thus, your initial objective is to provide free time which is reinforcing enough for them to work to meet your standards during the rest of the period.

(c) Make the contingencies clear: Take the time to explain to the class what you are doing. Let them understand the activities available during free time and the amount of free time available. State clearly the types of behaviors for which you intend to reduce their access to free time. It is probably a good idea to repeat the contingencies every morning for the first few days at least. If you change your free time

90

activities or change your rules, make the changes clear to everyone.

(d) Systematically deduct from the available free time for each pre-specified inappropriate behavior. Don't make exceptions. Write a big "15" where everyone can see it, and deduct one minute immediately after each violation , taking care not to make any comments other than possibly to state the violation.

POST-TEST OVER RESPONSE COST

1. Define response cost.

2. Under what circumstances should you use response cost to weaken undesirable behavior?

3. Give three examples of student behaviors which could be dealt with by the technique of response cost.
   (a)
   (b)
   (c)

4. In your eighth grade math class you are having trouble with students not completing their in-class assignments. Some students do all the work, some only partly complete it, and one of two never even start. The students are not particularily disruptive -- they just don't do much work. In order to apply RESPONSE COST WITH INDI-VIDUAL CONTINGENCIES in which the students are given the opportunity to earn reinforcement for appropriate behavior but reinforcers are systematically deducted for inappropriate behavior:
   (a) What reinforcement would you utilize?

(b) When would you make it available?

(c) How would you keep track of the amount of reinforcement available to each student? Give a
brief description of how this record system would
work.

(d) How and for what would you reduce access to the
available reinforcement? What would the "cost"
be?

(e) What are at least four desirable behaviors which
you might reinforce?
(1)
(2)
(3)
(4)
(5)

5. If you had two or three students in your <u>fourth grade</u>
who used profanity in their conversations with each
other, what would be the most appropriate technique for
weakening this behavior?

6. If you encountered a large number of students in your
<u>ninth grade</u> Social Studies class who frequently used
profanity, what would be the most appropriate technique
for weakening this behavior?

7. It seems as though it happens at least ten times a day.
You tell everyone exactly what you want them to do and
then you ask if there are any questions. In addition,
you usually ask if everyone is sure that he understands.

Invariably, the class is a silent sea of nodding little heads (hopefully nodding in agreement and not in sleep). But just as invariably, within ten minutes someone is at your desk asking what they were supposed to do.

(a) Which of the techniques which we have covered is most appropriate for weakening the behavior of asking the teacher several times to repeat directions?

(b) How would you apply the technique to this situation?

8. What are three variations of response cost which might be applied in the classroom?
(a)

(b)

(c)

9. Give an example of each of these three variations.
(a)

(b)

(c)

10. What are two reasons for employing group contingencies?
(a)
(b)

11. What are the differences between individual and group contingencies in terms of:

    (a) Who is fined for inappropriate behavior?

    (b) Logistics?

12. What are two ways to prevent a student from losing more reinforcers than arc available to him?

    (a)

    (b)

TECHNIQUE V: PUNISHMENT

OBJECTIVES:

(1)   You will be able to define punishment, stating that it
is the presentation of some stimulus which decreases
the likelihood of the preceding response's recurring.

(2)   You will be able to tell under what circumstances you
should use punishment to weaken undesirable behavior.

(3)   You will be able to give three examples of responses
which could be dealt with by punishment.

(4)   You will be able to write two adverse side effects of
using punishment.

(5)   You will be able to write how to judge whether an
environmental event is punishing or reinforcing.

(6)   You will be able to give at least three examples of
teacher and principal responses which are often
ineffective as punishment because they are in some
way reinforcing to students.

(7)   You will be able to tell under what conditions the
adverse side effects of punishment are most pronounced.
These are when:
(a)   punishment is delivered in a sarcastic, abusive
manner
(b)   punishment is directed not at specific student
behavior, but at the student himself

(8)   You will be able to tell when your verbal punishment
is usually most effective. This is when the majority
of your interaction with students is positive.

(9)   Given a classroom situation in which a teacher is
attempting to modify a student's behavior by the use
of punishment, you will be able to point out errors
in the teacher's application of this concept. The
errors will involve:
(a)   Breaking one or more of the four rules for weakening undesirable behavior
(b)   Breaking one or more of the five rules for using
reinforcers

(c) Reacting in a sarcastic, abusive, or emotional manner

(d) Interpreting the brief suppression of a behavior as effective punishment

(e) Attempting to weaken undesirable behavior by a consequence thought to be punishing, but which in reality is reinforcing

(10) Given a classroom situation in which one or more students are exhibiting undesirable behavior, you will be able to describe how to use punishment to effect some desired change in the students' behavior.

WHAT IS PUNISHMENT?

(1) Punishment is the <u>presentation of some stimulus which decreases the likelihood of the response which precedes it.</u> Potential types of punishment are scolding, spanking, frowning, and poor grades.
By definition, then, punishment differs from reinforcement in that punishment _____ the likelihood of the preceding response whereas reinforcement _____ the likelihood of the preceding response.

*decreases
 increases

(2) Like reinforcers, punishers vary from individual to individual and from time to time with the same person. The anger of the teacher might be punishment for one learner, but _____ for another.

*reinforcement

(3) Scolding does not punish the child who wants attention nor does being sent home punish the child who _____ _____.

*hates school

(4) Thus, whenever you decide to punish a student, you should make sure that what you intend to do will be perceived by that student as _____.

*punishment

96

(5) As we do with reinforcement, we judge whether an
environmental event is punishing by the effect which
it has on behavior. Probably the easiest way to
ascertain whether the likelihood of a response is
being decreased or increased is to observe its frequency of occurrence. Thus, if you react to a student's
behavior and the behavior is decreased in frequency,
then your reaction was probably _____.

*punishing

(6) If you tell a student repeatedly to "Be quiet," and he
persists in talking, your reaction (was, was not)
_____ punishing because the behavior did
not decrease in _____.

*was not
 frequency

(7) If the student not only keeps talking but talks more
often than before, it is possible that your scolding
is _____ the behavior.

*reinforcing

WHEN SHOULD YOU USE PUNISHMENT?

(1) Punishment should be used ONLY when the other methods
of weakening inappropriate behavior prove unsuccessful.
Thus, punishment should be viewed as a last _____
in dealing with inappropriate behaviors.

*resort

(2) To punish students less or to be more approving than
disapproving is not tantamount to permissiveness. What
is implied is that there are better ways to lessen
disruptive behavior and to strengthen academic behavior
than by _____.

*punishment, disapproval

WHY SHOULD PUNISHMENT BE YOUR LAST RESORT IN DEALING WITH
BEHAVIOR PROBLEMS?

Though properly applied punishment can often cause a
dramatic decrease in the frequency and intensity of undesirable behavior, this method has at least two AVERSIVE

97

CONSEQUENCES which negate any short term gains:

(A) If the student is subjected to frequent aversive consequences for his behavior, the teacher, the school, and
even the educational process itself may become aversive
to him.

   (1) Conversely, the person or system which provides
        reinforcement will probably become _____
        to the student.

        *reinforcing

   (2) Hence, in comparison with a teacher who provides
        considerable social reinforcement for her pupils,
        we would expect a teacher who is strongly asso-
        ciated with aversive consequences to be _____.

        *less reinforcing, less effective

   (3) It seems that many teachers have had the idea that
        aversive control could be used to persuade the
        student to learn something, but that after he left
        school the natural contingencies would take over
        and reinforce him for using what he had learned.
        In other words, the student would find that what
        he was forced to learn is indeed very useful.
        However, this type of control backfires because
        some aspects of school become so distasteful that
        the individual totally shuns that type of material
        when he is released from his forced study. Thus,
        kids are so "turned off" to education that the
        natural contingencies don't sustain the knowledge
        (assuming that the student acquired some knowledge
        in the first place) because the mechanics of gain-
        ing and implementing knowledge in this area have
        become _____ to him.

        *aversive

   (4) If one of the functions of the school system is to
        equip the student with both the academic skills
        and the desire to continue his education through-
        out his life, it would seem to be self-defeating
        for it to become strongly associated with aversive
        experiences. In comparison with someone who has
        met a good deal of frustration and defeat in the
        classroom, the student who has had positive

98

experiences is _____ likely to study on his own after he has completed his formal education.

*more

(5) However, the effect of aversive consequences on the behavior of the student while he is still in school is of more immediate (though not lesser) importance. When someone is subjected to punishing consequences for his behavior, he attempts to escape these consequences. In the classroom, behaving appropriately or doing satisfactory work are ways of _____ from punishment and disapproval.

*escaping

(6) Unfortunately, they are NOT always the most accessible or the most rewarding ways. The teacher's disapproval and the poor grades can be avoided by quitting school, cutting class, cheating, lying, or simply by not getting caught. Thus, ANY behavior which is successful in avoiding aversive consequences is _____.

*reinforced

(B) Another major disadvantage of punishment is that the teacher who frequently resorts to physical and verbal attacks to deal with problems is providing a poor role model for the learner.

(1) One of the most accepted functions of the teacher is to provide a good model of conduct for pupils. Few educators wish to teach their students to solve their problems through physical and verbal aggression, yet this is precisely what they are attempting to do when they spend much of their day verbally and physically _____ their pupils (often in some pretty abusive language).

*punishing

Teaching a lifelong commitment to learning?

(2) It is not surprising that students who imitate a
     punitive teacher will begin to deal with their own
     problems in a _____ manner.

     *punitive

CORRECT APPLICATION OF PUNISHMENT:

(1) Punishment is _____
     _____.

     *the presentation of some stimulus which decreases the
        likelihood of the preceding response's recurring.

(2) In the unit on positive reinforcement we placed great
     emphasis on the fact that any form of teacher attention,
     even attention which the teacher intends to be aversive,
     can be _____.

     *reinforcing

(3) The only way that you can tell whether your reaction is
     reinforcing or punishing is to observe the effect which
     it has on the _____ of the student's
     behavior.

     *frequency

(4) If a teacher has been chastising a 2nd grader for
     having temper tantrums and the child continues to have
     about two tantrums per day (and always has had two per
     day), it would seem that the teacher's efforts are not
     _____ the behavior, and might even be
     _____ it.

     *punishing
      reinforcing, maintaining

(5) We can tell that the teacher was not punishing the
     behavior because the tantrums did not decrease in
     _____.

     *frequency

(6) But we have a problem here. Maybe the child quietens
     down when the teacher chastises him. If this happens,
     the teacher might feel that her reaction has been
     effective because it has stopped the disruptive

behavior. But there is another way to look at it. Maybe she has just given the child what he wanted (attention), and he has no more reason to scream. In other words she has just let him know that any time that he wants attention, he can _____.

*throw a tantrum and get it

(7) Anyone who is skeptical of contingency management should watch the kids -- they are experts at it. If they find that your positive attention is not accesible, they will work to get your _____ attention.

*negative

(8) Hence, you should observe MORE than the immediate effects of your reaction. You should observe the _____ of the behavior through a specific period of _____ (e.g., disruptions per day or disruptions per class period) and over a period of days.

*frequency
 time

(9) If you find yourself telling the same student to "Be a little quieter", or to "Sit down", several times each day, then you might conclude that these verbal reactions are not really _____ and that you should look for new _____ for dealing with these problems.

*punishment
 strategies, methods

(10) Thus, one of the problems of making extensive use of punishment in the classroom is the difficulty of finding effective punishers. Our concern over this point is reflected in our emphasis on the frequent dichotomy between teacher and pupil perceptions of the teacher's reactions to student behaviors. For example, students may resent being told to "shut up", but they may prefer almost any type of teacher attention to _____ _____.

*being ignored

(11) Probably the best example of this is the common practice of "punishing" learners by suspending them. If
a student is humiliated by constant criticism and is
told only what is wrong with his behavior, the school
will become _____ to him. You might be
punishing him by making it hard for him to catch up
with his work and by making it more difficult for him
to get his diploma (an ethically questionable practice
at best), but you are also reinforcing him by removing

_____
_____.

*aversive
   him from the aversive consequences of everyday school
      life

(12) By definition, a punisher reduces the frequency of the
preceding behavior. Yet careful observation of most
classrooms indicates that the majority of actions
which the teachers view as punishment do not decrease
the frequency of classroom disruptions. We might
conclude from this observation that some teachers are
not utilizing _____.

*effective punishers

(13) Being sent to the principal's office might be aversive
to some students -- certainly few people perceive the
physical pain of a spanking as reinforcement. But
there are other factors. Often a student who is
painfully disciplined by the principal is looked upon
as "tough" by other students. Someone who doesn't
turn in his homework is reprimanded by the teacher, but
is praised by other students who also failed to do
their work. Thus, it is difficult to find effective
punishers in the classroom environment because much of
what teachers and principals attempt to _____
is some way _____ by other students.

*punish
   reinforced

(14) The aversive side effects of punishment are most
pronounced when the punishment is delivered in a
sarcastic or abusive manner. Thus, not only should
you follow the rule for weakening undesirable behavior
which states that you should direct your response at

_____,

103

but you should be especially careful to avoid _____
_____ responses.

*specific student behaviors, not at the student himself
sarcastic or abusive

(15) Punishment should be delivered in as matter-of-fact
way as possible, telling the student what he has done
wrong and what the consequences are. For example,
"Bob, I saw you break that window. You are going to
have to work out some way to pay for it." A statement such as this does not abuse Bob's character or
make a moral judgement on his actions. It is a simple
statement of what the inappropriate behavior was and
what the _____ of this behavior are.

*consequences, effects

(16) If you are only verbally rebuking a student (as we
have noted earlier, if most of your interaction with
students is positive, your rare negative reactions
will probably be perceived as punishment), you might
speak in terms of what he has done wrong and the
effect which this behavior has had on you or on his
classmates. For example, "Sandy, I am really dis-
appointed that you said that to Mr. Jones," or
"Bob, your loud talking is making it hard for everyone else to work." You are still giving the student
feedback on the _____ of his behavior without making broad statements which attack _____
_____.

*consequences
the student himself, the character of the student

(17) Also, it is better to avoid warnings and threats such
as "If I ever catch you doing that again, I am going
to . . ." or "You had better never let me see that
again." Students soon learn how much they can do
and elicit nothing more than a warning. Usually this
amounts to the same teacher warning the same student
not to do the same thing each day. It is preferable
to make a clear statement of the contingencies to
everyone and then to follow through on every violation.
For example, "Anyone whose desk has writing or carving
on it will have to stay in during recess and scrub
his and three other desks with steel wool, soap, and
water." Thus, _____ should understand

104

the contingencies. No student is forced to misbehave
to find out what the _____ are.

*everyone
contingencies

(18) If at all possible, the punishment should involve
      reparation for the offense, or at least be related in
      some way to the offense. This axiom is particularily
      pertinent when destruction of property is involved.
      If feasible, the student should pay for the damage
      or repair it himself. A student who takes screws out
      of desks might have to _____. An
      additional, related punishment might be to have him
      tighten the screws on _____.

*replace these screws
all of the desks in the room

(19) However, since many students would prefer to be tight-
      ening screws than working math problems, it might be
      a good idea to have this type of reparation occur
      at a time when it is aversive to the student. So
      rather than let the student tighten all of the screws
      during class, you might have him do it (when?) _____
      _____.

*during recess, free time, activities period, after
    school, etc.

THINK ABOUT THE FOLLOWING INCIDENT IN TERMS OF WHAT YOU
HAVE LEARNED ABOUT PUNISHMENT.

        Charles M. has been giving Ms. Johnston problems all
year. He gets along poorly with the other students and
seldom does my work. Ms. Johnston has tried everything
she can think of to interest Charles in his work, and even
more just to keep him from fighting. She finally decides
to concentrate on just one of Charles' problems at a time.
Accordingly, she wants to stop his fighting. Since the
fighting cannot be ignored and positive reinforcement of
desired behavior alone is not enough, she tries time-out.
Not surprisingly, Charles is so disgusted with school that
he seems to thrive on time-out. Finally, Ms. Johnston
tells him that any time that he fights he will be punished
severely. Not fifteen minutes later, Charles shoves over
Tommy's desk. Ms. Johnston is furious--she rushes to the

rear of the room, grabs Charles by the arm, and pulls him into the hall. There she proceeds to lecture him on how evil he is and how he will be severely punished if he ever fights again. The next day Charles kicks Bill. Ms. Johnston immediately sends Charles home.

WHICH OF THE FOLLOWING ERRORS DID MS. JOHNSTON MAKE IN APPLYING THE CONCEPT OF PUNISHMENT?
(Choose one or more of the following; answers are below)

(a) She did not give the punishment immediately after the undesired behavior.
(b) She did not make sure that what she perceived to be punishment would also be considered punishment by the student.
(c) She did not impress Charles with the disadvantages of using punishment.
(d) She did not make the contingencies clear to Charles.
(e) She was inconsistent.

ANSWER

b,d,e

EXPLANATION

(a) She was immediate in her punishment.

(b) Though Ms. Johnston would feel punished if someone scolded her or sent her home, the scolding is probably water off the proverbial duck's back to Charles. In fact, he might even relish the attention, i.e., scolding might be a positive reinforcer for him. Surely you would be reinforcing this student rather than punishing him by sending him home.

(c) The teacher should be aware of these disadvantages; not Charles.

(d) The contingencies weren't clear. What does she mean by "punished severely"? Does a student have to break a rule to find out the consequences?

(e) She warned one day and punished the next. It took days for Charles to find out that he would be punished sometimes. He should have found out the first day that he would be punished each time that he fought.

POST-TEST OVER PUNISHMENT

1. Define punishment.

2. What are two adverse side effects of using punishment?
   (a)
   (b)

3. Under what circumstances should you use punishment?

4. Give three examples of responses which could be dealt
   with by punishment.
   (a)
   (b)
   (c)

5. While on lunchroom duty you observe one of the students
   in the cafeteria line actually throwing his plate of
   food onto the floor and yelling, "I'm not going to eat
   this slop." Though it might very well be slop, you have
   to do something.

   (a) Write at least three ways in which you might punish
       this student. They should in some way be related to
       the offense, i.e., don't make him run around the
       football field.
       (1)

       (2)

       (3)

   (b) After deciding on one of these "courses of action"
       (a nice way of saying "how to make him pay"),
       write exactly what you should <u>say</u> to this student.

6. When Ms. Bixby turned around she saw Susan copying from a small slip of paper stuck up the sleeve of her dress. Ms. Bixby immediately stopped writing on the board, rushed back to Susan's desk, and tore her paper to shreds. She then began to loudly lecture Susan, telling her how pointless copying was, that she was ashamed of her, that her parents would be ashamed of her, that she should know better, asking her if she didn't know any better, and why she couldn't do anything right.

What is the most flagrant error that Ms. Bixby has made in dealing with this problem?

7. When is verbal punishment most effective?

8. WHAT and WHEN do you observe in order to judge whether an environmental event is punishing or reinforcing?
   (a) What?

   (b) When?

9. Under what circumstances are the adverse side effects of punishment most pronounced?
   (a)
   (b)

10. What are at least three examples of teacher and principal responses which are often ineffective as punishment because they in some way result in reinforcement to students.
    (a)
    (b)
    (c)
    (d)

EPILOGUE

In reviewing the text, we find that have devoted much more attention to techniques for weakening undesirable behavior than to methods for strengthening desired behavior. This emphasis is unfortunate since the amount of time spent on those two topics should be reversed.

However, despite our disproportionate attention to procedures for weakening "bad" behavior, we would like to close the book with a special plea for increased teacher sensitivity to "good" behaviors. This plea is based on three considerations. First, no method of weakening undesired behavior can be wholly effective without concomitant reinforcement of desired behavior. If you want a student to behave appropriately, YOU MUST REINFORCE HIS APPROPRIATE BEHAVIOR. Telling a student what he has done wrong isn't enough. You must also tell him what he has done right. Therefore, regardless of how you go about weakening undesirable responses, it is essential that you concurrently reinforce desirable responses.

Second, if from the very outset you consistently reinforce students for behaving appropriately, you will find that very few bad behaviors even present themselves. In other words, positive reinforcement not only aids in the weakening of undesirable behavior, but it often obviates the necessity of dealing with inappropriate behaviors. You will prevent a "multitude of sins" if, from the very beginning, you give students ample attention when they are behaving appropriately.

Finally, the emphasis is misplaced simply because everyone seems to remember that teachers are paid to keep students quiet and out of trouble, but few recognize that teachers should also be paid to REWARD innovation, spontaneity, co-operation, attention, and academic productivity. It doesn't take much effort to tell a child to go to the time-out area or to sit down and be quiet. It is so easy to tell a pupil who has disobeyed you that he is going to lose 10 points, or that if he does not sit down he will not go to the play area. In fact, telling a student what he has done wrong or what he shouldn't do seems to be the easiest thing in the world for most of us. Certainly it is a rare person who consistently looks only for the good things that others do.

We recognize that attending primarily to good behaviors is not the most natural mode of operation. It is hard to go over to the pupil who argued with you yesterday and tell her that her book report this week is a big improvement over last week's, or that you like the way she answered the questions in class today. It is hard to remember to tell the sad looking little kid in the back of the room that you really appreciate his effort on last night's homework. It is so easy to notice the boisterous ones and the angelic do-gooders on the front row and to ignore everyone else until they do something exceptionally good or perniciously evil. In contrast, it takes conscious, hard work to regularly notice and acknowledge the achievements, however small, of all students.

Occasionally, though (if not inevitably), things go wrong. Even with your most sincere approval, your most dazzling charm, and your most neatly typed lesson plans, students do get into fights, disturb others with noise or activity, and fail to get work accomplished. When (if) this happens, you will probably feel compelled to take some action to decrease the inappropriate behavior. At this point we might re-emphasize that punishment should be the LAST, not the first action, that you consider in weakening the behavior.

Your first attempt, of course, should be simply to ask (not tell) your pupils to change their behavior. Assuming that this strategy is ineffective, your next consideration should be whether you can utilize a combination of extinction and reinforcement of incompatible behavior. As we pointed out in the text, if you are the source of reinforcement or if you have control over the reinforcement, this combination is often sufficient to eliminate undesirable behavior.

However, if you do not control the reinforcement, it will be necessary to employ reinforcement of incompatible behavior in combination with either time-out or response cost. If the students are not too old and if only a few are emitting the disruptive behaviors, you might wish to send them to time-out. However, if you're dealing with junior and senior high school students or if there are more disruptive students than you can realistically send to time-out at one time, response cost might be more appropriate. Response cost can be used in a number of different ways and constitutes one of the cleanest, most effective means for dealing with inappropriate behavior.

If all else fails or if it's absolutely impossible to implement any of the previous strategies, you MIGHT consider punishment. But bear in mind that even though punishment is probably the most commonly used method of classroom control, it is very difficult to implement properly and often has adverse side effects which negate any short term gains in classroom control. Among other things, you always run the risk of either making both yourself and school aversive to the students or of providing a punitive role model for your pupils.

Hence, you should make every effort to organize your classroom activities so that reinforcement of appropriate behavior is a frequent occurrence. Though it would be impossible to acknowledge every desirable behavior emitted by your students, it is certainly feasible to notice some of the appropriate behaviors exhibited by each student. In toto, when your pupils do something right, let them know that you appreciate it. They cannot read your mind-- they have to go by what you say and do.